MING SHU

THE ART AND PRACTICE OF CHINESE ASTROLOGY

DEREK WALTERS

A FIRESIDE BOOK
PUBLISHED BY SIMON & SCHUSTER, INC.
NEW YORK — LONDON — TORONTO — SYDNEY — TOKYO

THE AUTHOR

Derek Walters is one of the few practising specialists of
Chinese Astrology in the Western hemisphere.

Born in the Year of the Fire-Rat, during the Wood-season,
in a Dragon-month, he takes his opportunism from the
Rat, the Wood accounts for his creative side, and the Fire,
a scientific leaning; while the influence of the Dragon is
the stimulus for his interest in *Ming Shu*.

A Fireside Book
Published by Simon & Schuster, Inc.
Simon & Schuster Building
Rockefeller Center
1230 Avenue of the Americas
New York, New York 10020

FIRESIDE and colophon are registered
trademarks of Simon & Schuster, Inc.

Originally published in 1987
in Great Britain by Pagoda Books.

Printed and bound in Italy by Sagdos

1   3   5   7   9   10   8   6   4   2

Library of Congress Cataloging-in-Publication Data

Walters, Derek, 1936-
    Ming shu.
    "A Fireside book."
    Bibliography: p.
    Includes index.
    1. Astrology, Chinese.   I. Title.
BF1714.C5W24   1988   133.5   87-12158
ISBN 0-671-65246-X

CONTENTS

A SCHOLARLY DISCUSSION

The Emperor Yüan, wishing to choose an auspicious day
for his enthronement, summoned the sage T'ai Yang, and
the Grand Astrologer Ch'en Cho, to choose the day
which they deemed the most appropriate.

T'ai Yang selected the twenty-fourth day of the third
month, that being the day of the Third Stem and the
Seventh Branch. Ch'en Cho, however, disagreed,
proposing the twenty-second of the month, pertaining to
the First Stem and Fifth Branch. Said Ch'en Cho: "The
King of Yüeh, on the advice of the astrologer Fan Li, chose
such a day to return to his own land."

T'ai Yang declared: "Quite so. But the King of Yüeh had
been a prisoner of Emperor Wu, and was inwardly
rebellious. Fan Li chose such a day because the virtuous
influences were directed outward, while destructive
influences pointed at the centre, and so attacked the
palace of the Emperor Wu. Our own king has no such
inner resentment, and his throne is lawfully endowed by
Heaven."

The King carefully listened to the arguments of the two
philosophers, and accepted the advice proffered by the
sage T'ai Yang.

From *The History of the Chin Dynasty (c. AD300)*

"Doctors, Diviners and Magicians of Ancient China" by
Kenneth J. DeWoskin, Columbia University Press, 1983.

THE PLATES

The beautiful allegorical paintings, which have been specially commissioned to accompany the text of this book, not only portray the characteristics of the animal personalities in symbolic manner, but also depict the course of the seasons and the times of day appropriate to each sign.

The **Rat**, rescuing the bait without being trapped, hints at crafts and intellect, as also represented by the mathematical instruments shown, while dark shades reveal this to be the time of the Winter Solstice and also the double-hour of the Rat, around midnight. (Pages 16-17).

The philosopher, Lao Tzu, meanwhile, rides the slow but reliable **Ox**, with the Great Wall of China, symbol of stability and endurance, in the background. This is the second Chinese double-hour, and late winter. (Pages 20-21).

The Chinese New Year always falls in the Tiger month. Here, the powerful leap of the **Tiger** symbolises strength of purpose, change, and even revolution, as the commander of the Imperial forces plans his next move before dawn. (Pages 24-25).

The girl gathering herbs reveals the **Hare** to be the emblem of medicine, cosmetics, healing, and the elixir of youth, while the Spring equinox and the dawn hour are further symbolised by the appearance of the sun and moon together. (Pages 28-29).

The **Dragon**, blazoned on the walls of the palace, is the symbol of money and fortune, commerce and luck, represented by the market in the distance and the men playing dice in the foreground. The double-hour of the Dragon falls in early morning, and it is late spring. (Pages 32-33).

Disdaining the intrigues being plotted in the refinement of an elegant garden, perhaps only the mystic **Snake** knows the truth. The double-hour of the Snake falls in the late morning, and its season is early summer. (Pages 36-37).

The muted tones in which the **Horse** is portrayed remind us that this is high-noon in mid-summer, while the eager riders in this race symbolise competitiveness and courage. (Pages 40-41).

In contrast to the Horse, the **Sheep** symbolises the gentler side of human nature. It is the eighth double-hour in the early afternoon, and late summer, as the monks retire to contemplate the world beyond. (Pages 44-45).

Appropriately, an armillary sphere is used to symbolise the **Monkey**'s craft and technical skills. But mischief and humour are never far away, and the pompous Imperial secretary is about to lose his finest brush! It is late afternoon, the ninth double-hour, in early autumn. (Pages 48-49).

Pages 52-53 feature the splendid **Rooster**, symbol of the Autumn equinox, looking proudly on, as an elderly couple take their quiet leisure at sunset, aptly symbolised by the chrysanthemum. (*"What am I to do now?" sadly asked an elderly Empress, after her husband had taken a young concubine. "You are as a chrysanthemum in the autumn of my years," was the old man's tender reply.*)

Faithfulness and loyalty are shown by the **Dog** and his master, the watchman; while in the distance, migrating geese, as the *Book of Rites* teaches, reveal this to be the eleventh double-hour and the end of autumn. (Pages 56-57).

Finally, the cycle is brought to an end with a depiction of the contented **Pig**, symbol of happy domesticity, settling down to rest at the close of day. It is the twelfth double-hour, and the beginning of winter. (Pages 60-61).

'THUS SPAKE THE LORD GRAND ASTROLOGER:

"Since Man's earliest existence, through succeeding
generations, was there ever a time when the rulers failed to
observe the Sun, Moon, and Planets, record their motions, and
expound their meanings? Raise the head, and contemplate the
vastness of the Heavens; look round, and marvel at their
manifestations on Earth. Theirs is the primaeval force, and such
was related by the sages of long ago."'

*Ssu Ma Ch'ien, the first historian of China,
writing in the second century BC*

INTRODUCTION

In ancient China, no less than in the Western world, it was firmly believed that one's destiny was linked with the moment of birth. Events on Earth reflected those in Heaven; and if the actions of mankind — the temporary caretakers of this planet — were not in accordance with Heaven's mandate, then dire calamities would be the inevitable result.

Thus it was that the ancient Chinese sages — like their Western counterparts, the magicians and astrologers of Babylon — strove to unlock the secrets of Heaven and so foretell the outcome of earthly events from the location of the stars and planets.

But in those early times, astrological secrets were for the Emperor's court alone, and Heaven's portents were considered far too weighty for ordinary mortals. Every functionary at the Imperial court had his own particular star, revealing his own individual destiny; and the Emperor's, of course, was, as Confucius said, "the Pole Star, round which all the other stars make obeisance." Indeed, for anyone outside the Imperial circle, study of the movements of the stars was tantamount to treason, and punishable by death.

But as that vast empire expanded, ritual and ceremony took an increasingly important part in sustaining its ordered society. Accordingly, strict observation of the calendar and its associated functions became an integral part not only of court but of every-day social and family life, and a new art evolved — *Ming Shu* (in translation, literally, '*the reckoning of Fate*') by which Chinese astrology was brought to the people through the medium of the astronomically-regulated calendar.

In time, the astrologer began to play a role as central as that of a Registrar of Births, Marriages and Deaths, since it was principally on these occasions that he was consulted. He may have been the local fortune-teller, or an itinerant folk-doctor, whose visiting card declared him to be 'Expert in *Yin* and *Yang*, Earth Currents, Selecting Fortunate Days, and Telling Fortunes by the Four Pillars.' Just as likely, he was one of the priests from the local temple, whose revenues depended more on the casting of horoscopes than voluntary donations.

Even today, when a child is born, the Chinese astrologer notes the hour, day, month and year of birth (the Four Pillars of Fate) and thereby reveals the infant's destiny. Moreover, it is not unheard of for parents to give their babies away, particularly if they are girls, should the Four Pillars suggest that they would bring disgrace to the family. A story current among the Boat People from Vietnam tells that after the astrologically ill-timed arrival of a baby boy, the distraught parents turned to the grandfather for advice. The boy, however, was a bonny one; and seeing this, the sagacious patriarch announced that disgrace was less important than having a male heir. The parents took the advice to heart, and so the baby was saved.

Until very recently, too, marriages were seldom contracted between Chinese families unless astrologers had decreed that the Four Pillars of the two partners were entirely compatible. A young man had only to write the Four Pillars of his birth-date on the back of his card and present it to his prospective father-in-law for this to be accepted as a formal proposal of marriage.

It might be thought that after death, at least, concern for horoscopes would cease, but that was far from being the case. The astrologer was once again consulted, this time to find a day for the funeral which would be compatible with the Four Pillars of the deceased. This could mean that the ceremony would be days or weeks ahead, in which case discretion ruled that the coffin be disguised with sheaves of grass, to deceive the marauding gods of thunder and lightning. And should one of the funeral party have fallen ill, it was important to discover whether it was because the deceased had been offended in some way, or whether it was merely that the Four Pillars of the sick mourner were not in agreement with those of the departed.

On New Year's Day, modern Chinese families from Hong Kong to San Francisco, just like their forebears, either employ a professional astrologer, or, more likely, consult the Chinese Almanac to see what the coming year holds in store for them. In Hong Kong alone, a million copies of the Almanac are sold annually, among a population of five million. The Almanac contains daily directions for almost every conceivable action, from digging trenches to washing hair: and the Chinese give the closest attention to these instructions since, again, the penalties for ignoring them are believed to be as formidable in the next world as they are in this.

Young Chinese girls, in particular, are eager to know what kind of husband Fate has in store for them. Their special day is the Feast of the Double Seventh, on the seventh day of the seventh moon, when ancient tradition holds that magpies gather to form a bridge across the Milky Way, so that the Weaving Maiden can visit her lover, the Cow-herd. The Weaving Maiden is the patroness of unmarried girls, and on this day her subjects bring her various offerings and have their fortunes told, always hoping, of course, that this will be the last occasion when they will do so.

Clearly, astrology must have developed completely separately in the two ancient worlds, for the ways used by the Babylonians to study and catalogue the stars are quite different from those followed by the Chinese — not just in the matter of calculating the horoscopes, but even more importantly in their interpretations of the celestial phenomena.

At a popular level, the most striking point of departure is that Chinese astrology appears to base character assessments on the *year* of birth while, in the West, it is the *month* of birth that is the criterion. In each case, such a superficial view is misleading, and to consider either Chinese or Western astrology in these terms alone would be quite wrong. There are many other factors involved. The Chinese, for instance, attach particular importance to the Five Elements — Wood, Fire, Earth, Metal and Water — which, at different times in life, exert a considerable influence on personal fortune and happiness. Their importance, however, has to date usually only been touched upon in Western accounts of Chinese astrology, which tend to focus almost entirely on the Twelve Animal Cycle.

The twelve animals of Chinese astrology

The cycle of twelve years, each named after an animal, and often misleadingly called the 'Chinese Zodiac' was introduced only a thousand years ago, which in Chinese historical terms is comparatively recently. This most familiar aspect of Chinese astrology declares that, depending on the year of birth, an individual is either a *Rat* or an *Ox*: a *Tiger, Hare, Dragon, Snake, Horse, Sheep, Monkey, Rooster, Dog* or *Pig*.

Before these animal names were introduced, Chinese astrologers had reckoned the years by the 'Twelve Earthly Branches', originally used to mark the twelve years it takes the

planet Jupiter to complete its orbit of the sky: and the Chinese still call this cycle the 'Great Year', each month of which is one of our ordinary years.

But abstract concepts such as these numerical Branches are not easy for lay folk to understand. Accordingly, about a thousand years ago, and after Buddhism had become the dominant religion in China, those monks who were well-versed in the horoscopic arts replaced the Branches with the more easily remembered names of twelve animals, thus making astrology more accessible to ordinary people. How, or why, particular animals were chosen remains a mystery to this day: but popular legend tells that the Buddha named the years after those animals answering his summons.

The table on pages 84-88 lists the animal years for this century. Confusion frequently arises over their translation. The name of the second animal, *Niu*, (a generic term for cattle), could be translated as ox, buffalo, bull, or for that matter, even cow. Similarly, *Chu* might mean pig, boar, hog, or swine. It is important to remember, too, that Western animal symbolism often differs considerably from Chinese ideas. An individual may not feel particularly flattered, for example, to learn that he is a Rat-person or a Pig-person; but in China, the rat is regarded as the emblem of ingenuity, and the pig, the emblem of comfort.

The twelve animals and their houses

In Chinese tradition, the twelve animals are grouped into six pairs, the first of each pair having *yang* or active attributes; the second, softer *yin* qualities. In this way, the Rat is paired with the Ox; the Tiger with the Hare; the Dragon with the Snake; the Horse with the Sheep; the Monkey with the Rooster; and the Dog with the Pig.

These opposite poles of forces believed to permeate the physical and metaphysical universes are frequently thought of as being 'male' (*Yang*) and 'female' (*Yin*), but these are only terms of convenience. The two forces are in fact closer to the 'positive' and 'negative' polarites of physics: action and counter-action. If there is matter, there must be anti-matter; or, as the Chinese reasoned, thousands of years before Einstein, if there is existence, there must also be non-existence. *Yin* and *Yang* thus also represent the passive and active sides of the human character: creative as opposed to deductive processes, or physiologically, the left and right hemispheres of the brain.

Each of the six pairs of animals is also associated with one of six aspects of destiny known as 'Houses'. These influence the

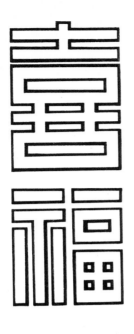

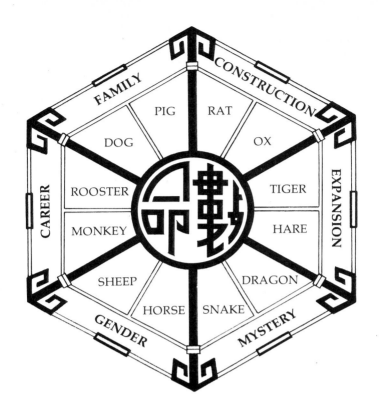

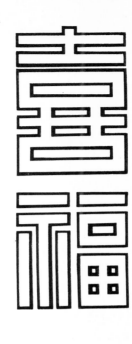

overall trends and general characteristics for the periods of time — years, months, days, or hours — associated with each animal. The Rat and the Ox, for example, are linked with the *House of Construction*, and during the Year of the Rat all new beginnings, concepts and births are favoured; whilst during the Year of the Ox, the omens are good for steady growth, leading to fruition and harvest. The Tiger and the Hare (in Vietnam, the Cat) are respectively the aggressive and diplomatic approaches in the *House of Expansion*; and in a sea of troubles, the one will take up arms, the other heal through moderation. The *House of Mystery* rules during the year of the exotic, alchemical Dragon and the year of the contemplative, secretive Snake. The *House of Gender* reveals the differences between the sexes, symbolised by the Horse and the Sheep, the former characterizing typically male forms of behaviour; the latter, female. The Monkey and the Rooster belong to the *House of Career*, wherein the one suggests progress through skill and technology, and the other through ambition and flair. Finally, the Dog, representing loyalty and protection, and the Pig, progeny and comfort, belong to the *House of Family*.

Accordingly, different periods of time favour different forms of conduct: there are times for innovation, spontaneity and risk; times too, for caution and reflection.

Personality revealed

Much of the appeal of astrology, both in the East and the West, lies in delineation of character and personality, something which often nudges its divinatory and predictive aspects into second place. In popular Chinese astrology, the animal-names of the twelve-yearly cycle are taken as direct indicators of personality: but why people take on the characteristics of the animal whose year they are born under, or how it was that the philosophers of old managed to categorise humanity into the twelve year-types, are matters for conjecture.

Those unfamiliar with Chinese astrological techniques may think this is an inherent weakness, for there would seem to be scant logic in a method which would apparently condemn all the students of a particularly inauspicious year to fail their examinations. And yet, this is perhaps one of the most demonstrably *positive* examples of Chinese astrology. How many teachers must have commented at some time that one year's particular intake differed from another! Thus, while the year-sign's qualities may not be readily apparent in a particular individual, its characteristics invariably become more evident in a group as a whole. As for the leaders, the geniuses, the clowns, and the misfits, what is it that makes certain people stand out from the rest of the crowd?

There are many ways in which each animal-type can be qualified to produce a more detailed character portrait, the general picture suggested by the animal of the year being modified by other birth-date factors. The twelve animal names are, for instance, also used in South-East Asia for twelve divisions of the day — the Rat, for example, corresponding to the double-hour 11pm - 1am, and the Horse to the double-hour 11am - 1 pm, as the table shows. Thus the time at which you were born is also relevant. Indeed, standard Chinese texts state that the hour of birth is fundamental to personality: and those who are familiar with Western astrology will know that the hour of birth provides the 'ascendant' of the horoscope, while in Chinese Astrology, it establishes the 'alter ego' — the real person trying to get out. Similarly, the animal names apply to twelve divisions of the year, and the month in which you were born has a bearing on the horoscope, too.

However, the Chinese months do not begin and end regularly on the same dates each year. Accordingly, the second table shown is only an approximate guide. To find out precisely in which animal month you were born, turn to Table IV on page 84-88. Here, for each year this century, can be found the dates for the first days of each Chinese month. Check your date of birth against these; and then, having looked at the top of the relevant column to ascertain the number of the month in which you were born, use the table provided here to find out your animal month.

**The Twelve Chinese Months
and their Associated Animals**

First month	approximating to February:	the Tiger
Second month	approximating to March:	the Hare
	(The Hare month includes the Spring Equinox)	
Third month	approximating to April:	the Dragon
Fourth month	approximating to May:	the Snake
Fifth month	approximating to June:	the Horse
	(The Horse month includes the Summer Solstice)	
Sixth month	approximating to July:	the Sheep
Seventh month	approximating to August:	the Monkey
Eighth month	approximating to September:	the Rooster
	(The Rooster month includes the Autumn Equinox)	
Ninth month	approximating to October:	the Dog
Tenth month	approximating to November:	the Pig
Eleventh month	approximating to December:	the Rat
	(The Rat month includes the Winter Solstice)	
Twelfth month	approximating to January:	the Ox

**The Twelve Chinese Double Hours
and their Ancient Names**

Double-hour of the Rat	11pm–1am	*Yeh Pàn*	Midnight
Double-hour of the Ox	1am –3am	*Chi Ming*	Cock-crow
Double-hour of the Tiger	3am –5am	*Ping Tan*	Nearly Dawn
Double-hour of the Hare	5am –7am	*Jih Ch'u*	Sunrise
Double-hour of the Dragon	7am –9am	*Shih Shih*	Meal-time
Double-hour of the Snake	9am –11am	*Yu Chung*	Before Noon
Double-hour of the Horse	11am–1pm	*Jih Chung*	Midday
Double-hour of the Sheep	1pm –3pm	*Jih Tieh*	Sun Declines
Double-hour of the Monkey	3pm –5pm	*Pu Shih*	Afternoon
Double-hour of the Rooster	5pm –7pm	*Jih Ju*	Sunset
Double-hour of the Dog	7pm –9pm	*Huang Hun*	Yellow Dusk
Double-hour of the Pig	9pm –11pm	*Jen Ting*	Repose

Compatibility between the animal types

Once you have discovered your own animal sign, you will no doubt want to know the signs of others close to you, and then to establish the nature and extent of the compatibility between friends and colleagues. There are two ways of doing this.

The first is purely objective, calculated according to the numerical relationships of different years, and can be demonstrated quite simply. If the names of the twelve animals are placed in order at the twelve hour-positions of a clock-face, with the birth-year animal at the twelve o'clock position, then the most compatible signs will be at four o'clock and eight o'clock, moderately compatible signs at two and ten o'clock, poorly compatible signs at three and nine o'clock, and adversity shown at six. The illustration on the cover to this book and also on page 65 shows the animals grouped according to these compatibilities.

Many folk-sayings, however, seem to contradict this neatly defined system. Throughout South-East Asia, for instance, there is a general distrust of girls born in the Year of the Tiger, no matter what the other person's natal animal. Moreover, there seems to be no general explanation for some other firmly established beliefs regarding compatibility, such as 'Rooster and Snake — ever at odds' which, theoretically, is a harmonious relationship; or, conversely, why folklore decrees that the Snake and the Hare make a supremely ideal couple.

Some of the reasoning, but obviously not all, lies in the second method of judging compatibility between animal signs, which is to consider the twelve types as representatives of actual beasts in nature. A horse, for example, gets on quite happily with most other domestic animals. Dogs and horses, once they have got over their mutual suspicion, make happy stable companions. Horses and sheep are friendly enough; and although they may not perhaps strike up the same rapport with members of the bovine community, rarely is there outward aggression. The subjective interpreter of an 'animal-charted' horoscope might say, therefore, of a Horse native, that a friendly relationship could be struck up with a Tiger or Hare personality after some mutual distrust; that there would be a harmonious relationship with a Sheep; a good working relationship with a Dog; and off-handed indifference to the Ox.

Such a rule-of-thumb guide, though perhaps seemingly fanciful, is generally easier to remember than the relationships between numbers or 'cyclical signs': and considering the twelve personality-types to be represented by the actual animals can be a useful *aide-memoire* in determining the various forms of personal interaction which might exist between different people.

The Five Elements

In order to make a more specific comparison of two personalities and thereby to determine their compatibility, however, it is also important to take into account the interaction of the Five Elements.

The Chinese hold that Five Elements — Wood, Fire, Earth, Metal and Water — rule the cycles of the Universe. Each produces the next in a generative order. (Wood burns, producing Fire; Fire leaves ash or Earth from which Metal is mined; Metal melts, like Water, which in turn feeds growing Wood; after which the whole cycle begins again.)

In this way, the year progresses through five seasons, each also associated with one of the Elements. The season of growth and creation is Wood; that of heat is Fire; the middle of the year is Earth; the harvest, Metal; and the cold, wet season, Water. And just as each Element is associated with a certain season, so each year, day and hour is also ascribed to one of the Five Elements. Indeed, at the moment of an individual's birth, there are stated to be twelve different all-important factors, each influenced by one of the Five Elements: and the profile of these combined elements is believed to shape an individual's character, personality and even fortune.

Popular accounts of Chinese astrology, however, tend to concentrate only on the Element associated with the *year*. In this way, someone born in 1945 is described as a 'Wood-Rooster', because the element associated with 1945 is Wood. Such an approach does not really do justice either to the importance of the Elements or their true significance, ignoring as it does all the Elements associated with the other Pillars: the month, day and hour. These other Elements are just as important as the Element for the year; and collectively they will yield a far deeper and more detailed personality portrait.

This is one of the most important aspects of the art and practice of Chinese Astrology, and is elaborated fully in the final, very practical section of this book which presents a step-by-step guide to casting and interpreting a Chinese horoscope.

As a general rule, two Elements which stand in the generative order (Wood — Fire — Earth — Metal — Water) are compatible, for one Element generates the other. But there is also a 'destructive' order (Wood — Earth — Water — Fire — Metal) in which each successive element overpowers the other, and such combinations are less fortunately placed. (Wood absorbs the goodness from Earth, which sullies Water, which quenches Fire, which melts Metal, which chops down Wood.)

From these two orders, it should not be difficult to estimate how a particular Element-type might help or hinder another. In the generative order, a Wood-person would provide the Fire-person with ideas; the Fire-type would stimulate the obstinate Earth; Earth gives stability to the rash Metal-type; Metal gives active support to the dreaming Water-personality, and Water provides the background information by means of which a Wood-personality is able to create.

Conversely, the Wood-type may well be a drain on the reserve of an Earth-personality; the Earth-personality could damage the Water-type's reputation; Water might quench Fire's enthusiasm; Fire would be a formidable opponent for the normally assertive Metal-type, who in turn might harrass the Wood-personality physically.

The Ten Heavenly Stems

The Chinese, as already explained, traditionally number their hours, days, months and years by the Twelve Earthly Branches; and these have, in popular reckoning, been replaced by the twelve animal names. But the Chinese also have a second cycle of calendar numbers called the *Ten Heavenly Stems*; and Chinese calendars, certainly the world's oldest in continuous use, still employ the Stems and Branches, thus preserving a tradition going back several thousands of years.

When you come to the final part of this book and find out how to cast your own horoscope, you will meet these Ten Stems again; but for the moment it is simply worth noting that, just as the Twelve Branches became known by the animal names, so the Ten Stems were superseded by the names of the Five Elements, running in pairs. Thus, Stems one and two are Wood; Stems three and four, Fire; five and six, Earth; seven and eight, Metal; nine and ten, Water.

Changes in fortune or personality

Much of what I have said so far may give the impression that, according to Chinese astrology, a person's character is decreed immutably from the womb to the tomb. Yet it frequently happens that we undergo partial or complete changes of fortune or personality. Of course, these changes may be due to outside pressures, or to the natural ripening of age and experience. Those who are usually bright and cheerful may, for example, become subject to bouts of depression through illness or personal loss, while normally quiet and reserved individuals, released from some onerous burden of responsibility, may suddenly take on a new lease of life. Such transformations are perfectly natural, and do not need astrology, Chinese or otherwise, to explain them.

But besides such understandable changes, there are often others which are less explicable, with no identifiable cause, but leading to equally significant transformations of character and behaviour in relationships. Astrologically, these changes are revealed in a *Life-Cycle Chart*, which maps the shifts in balance between the Five Elements over the course of time.

Chinese astrologers aver that these events can be foreseen by plotting the progress of the Elements — whether they are dominant, recessive, waxing or waning — throughout life. Thus, by noting which harmonics of the Five Elements will come to bear during infancy, childhood, schooldays, college, marriage, and maturity, the Chinese astrologer can advise on the best direction to take at vital stages in life.

You will find that Chinese astrology is an absorbing art. Certainly, its mysteries have captivated me for as long as I can remember. It is my hope that this book — with its superb, specifically commissioned colour plates by Nicholas Hewetson — will give every reader a deeper insight into what is an utterly fascinating yet previously little-explored subject.

DEREK WALTERS

THE TWELVE ANIMALS

Ancient Chinese astrologers observed that events on Earth tend to
follow a twelve-year pattern. They noticed, too, that those born in
the same year often share certain basic personality traits: and, once
this had been firmly established, named each of the twelve years
after an animal most closely epitomising its salient characteristics.

Thus, symbolically, according to the year in which each of us was
born, we are either a Rat, a Rooster, an Ox or a Tiger; a Horse, a
Dragon, a Sheep or a Pig; a Dog, a Hare, a Monkey or a Snake.

What, then, of the Rooster's personality? What might you expect of
the Monkey? And how is the Ox likely to fare in the Year of the Tiger?
The following pages provide a wealth of fascinating insight into the
animal symbolism that forms part of *Ming Shu*.

THE RAT PERSONALITY

In any description of the Rat-personality, the key-word is 'charm'. Indeed, anyone who begrudges being thought of as a Rat can take heart from the fact that, in Chinese, the word for rat is also used for mouse, mole, hamster, and several other small furry creatures.

The Rat is adaptable and creative, not lacking in flair or inventiveness. But, quick-witted, bright and sociable, the Rat also tends towards ostentatiousness and name-dropping in pursuit of what is today often euphemistically called 'upward mobility'.

The Rat's outward personality is certainly appealing: but below the surface there often abides a crafty and opportunist character, who tends to 'use' friends before eventually losing or dropping them, for one reason or another.

In financial matters, Rat-personalities are erratic; scrimping, cutting corners, and budgeting carefully when money is scarce, but spending lavishly instead of saving in times of plenty.

Bright and gregarious, with a well-developed taste for gossip, the Rat's intellectual versatility is not always immediately apparent. In particular, Rats have a remarkable command of abstract notions, such as numbers, and in a business situation they make great planners, especially when detailed and complex calculations are involved.

THE SYMBOLISM OF THE RAT 鼠

The Rat begins the procession of the Twelve Animals which give their names to the twelve units of the Great Year. The ancient sign for this year, *Tzu*, means 'infant' and signifies the beginning of a new era. This same sign is thus also used for the midnight hour of the Chinese clock, announcing the birth of a new day. At this time, the most active creatures are rats and mice; and perhaps because of this, the first hour of the day became known as the Rat hour.

Rats are actually venerated by some Chinese who believe that if certain rats can be persuaded to stay, they will guard the house against intruders, as might a dog. Indeed, the arrival of a particularly fat rat is welcomed with great glee, for the 'money rat' only visits a house where food is likely to be plentiful.

YEARS OF THE RAT
and their associated elements

31 Jan 1900 – 18 Feb 1901	*Metal*
18 Feb 1912 – 5 Feb 1913	*Water*
5 Feb 1924 – 23 Jan 1925	*Wood*
24 Jan 1936 – 10 Feb 1937	*Fire*
10 Feb 1948 – 28 Jan 1949	*Earth*
28 Jan 1960 – 14 Feb 1961	*Metal*
15 Feb 1972 – 2 Feb 1973	*Water*
2 Feb 1984 – 19 Feb 1985	*Wood*
19 Feb 1996 – 6 Feb 1997	*Fire*

THE YEAR OF THE RAT

From ancient times, Chinese astronomers reckoned the passing of years by an imaginary pointer in the sky called the T'ai Sui or Year-marker. It moved round the Heavens like the hour-hand of a cosmic clock, reaching its original starting-point every twelfth year, in the Year of the Rat.

Since the Year of the Rat begins the cycle of the Twelve Animals, it is regarded as the most auspicious time to inaugurate new plans, and to expand into new fields of development. Little activity may be seen on the surface; but at the heart of things, all kinds of changes are being planned. An idle notion may even suddenly become a revolutionary idea, for this is a time of intensely creative activity; a time when new horizons loom into view, bringing the startling realisation that a thousand possibilities have not been tried.

This is the time for new methods, fresh plans, and projects for re-organisation and re-vitalisation to be discussed. There may be opposition and scepticism later, but now is the moment to draft schemes in outline.

On the international front, Rat Years (in the present century, all those years of which the last two digits can be divided by twelve — 1960, 1972, 1984 for instance) are seldom remarkable. Historians, however, may argue that the seeds of some devastating world upheaval were sown during the Rat Year through an apparently trivial but nonetheless highly significant action.

Where health is concerned, the start of another cycle produces renewed vitality. Minor complaints should clear up, while more serious problems are stabilised. In matters of romance, this is marked as a good year for virtually everyone. Those without partners are likely to find them, while the settled could expect additions to the family, either children or grandchildren.

HOW EACH ANIMAL FARES IN THE RAT-YEAR

The Rat 鼠

The Year of the Rat begins the twelve-year animal cycle; and for the person fortunate enough to be born during the Rat Year, the time is ripe for new projects and fresh ventures. This is a good time for the Rat native to change houses, start a different job, or even to get involved in a new love affair. Finances are secured; and with regards to health, there will be a feeling of renewed fitness. A word of caution, though: next year may have a few difficult moments, and it would be sensible to try and salt away some of this year's gains.

The Ox 牛

The Ox is the complementary sign of the Rat, whose year this is: and while the Rat is the sign of creative activity, the Ox represents quiet accumulation. Generally this is a good year for investment for the Ox, rather than the development of projects which require active participation. In health matters, those who may have problems relating to their bones or joints should find improvement in their condition. Romantic attachments formed this year are unlikely to be long-lasting.

The Tiger 虎

The astrological charts reveal the Rat Year to be harmonious with the Tiger-section of the sky; yet despite this, the Rat Year is frequently bad for the Tiger, especially financially. On the bright side, however, there is every indication that it could be a good year for self-promotion or for social activity; and while both of these areas may make a heavy drain on the Tiger's resources, the outlay will repay dividends eventually.

The Hare 兔

The Rat Year is badly aspected with the Hare sector of the sky and does not augur well for those born in the Year of the Hare. It is important to watch finances, and health, too, could prove a problem, with an additional danger from accidental injury. But the Rat Year is nevertheless a year of innovation, and this may well be a good time for the Hare to inaugurate some new scheme, provided that financial commitment is kept at a modest level.

The Dragon 龍

This is an excellent year for the Dragon native, whose natural extrovert personality harmonises superbly with the innovative and creative Rat. It is an ideal time to open up a new line of activity. Business, romance and health are at their best. Take advantage of the wealth of opportunities the year has to offer.

The Snake 蛇

A time of steady progress for the Snake, the Rat Year, with its creative push, should be used to its fullest advantage in what is otherwise a calm and uneventful period. It would be wise to try and resolve any outstanding problems, in order to extract the maximum benefits from the excellent year which follows.

The Horse 馬

The Year-Marker is now directly opposite the sector of the sky which rules the Horse, making this most difficult period for the Horse-native, especially if there are to be dealings with people born in the Year of the Rat, who are now at their peak. There could be problems with expenditure, while personal relationships might also falter. Health, too, needs to be watched. This is definitely not a time for unnecessary risk.

The Sheep 羊

The New Year heralds a quiet, dormant period for those born during the Year of the Sheep — welcome news, for although the previous year was marked by progress and activity, a time of respite is needed now. The Rat Year provides an opportunity for steady growth and a strengthening of business and personal relationships, while health matters show little change.

The Monkey 猴

One of the best possible times for the person born in the Year of the Monkey, this is a year for invention, ideas, new proposals, and expansion. Not only do the Monkey and Rat sectors harmonise astrologically, but the creative impulse which springs up during the Rat Year is exactly the right kind of stimulus that the Monkey needs. There are excellent prospects in both business and romance, and physical fitness is at a peak.

The Rooster 鶏

This will be an adverse year for the Rooster. The Rat gnaws away at reserves, and the punctilious Rooster will not enjoy having to break into carefully saved funds. During this difficult period, it is advisable to take the greatest care in entering partnerships of either a business or romantic nature.

The Dog 犬

This is a good year for those born in the Year of the Dog; not one of the best, but better than usual. The Rat Year, being the start of the twelve-year cycle, brings about growth and expansion, and the Dog will benefit by investigating all the possibilities that this very positive period has to offer.

The Pig 豬

The Year of the Rat is a somewhat unstable time for the Pig-native, who will have found the previous year to be one characterised by a sense of completion and fulfilment. Now, however, comes a time of upheaval, relocation and re-organisation: and although the signs are not particularly adverse, there will be resentment over frustrated ambitions. Apart from such disconcerting changes, the year will have other rewards in the fresh opportunities it brings.

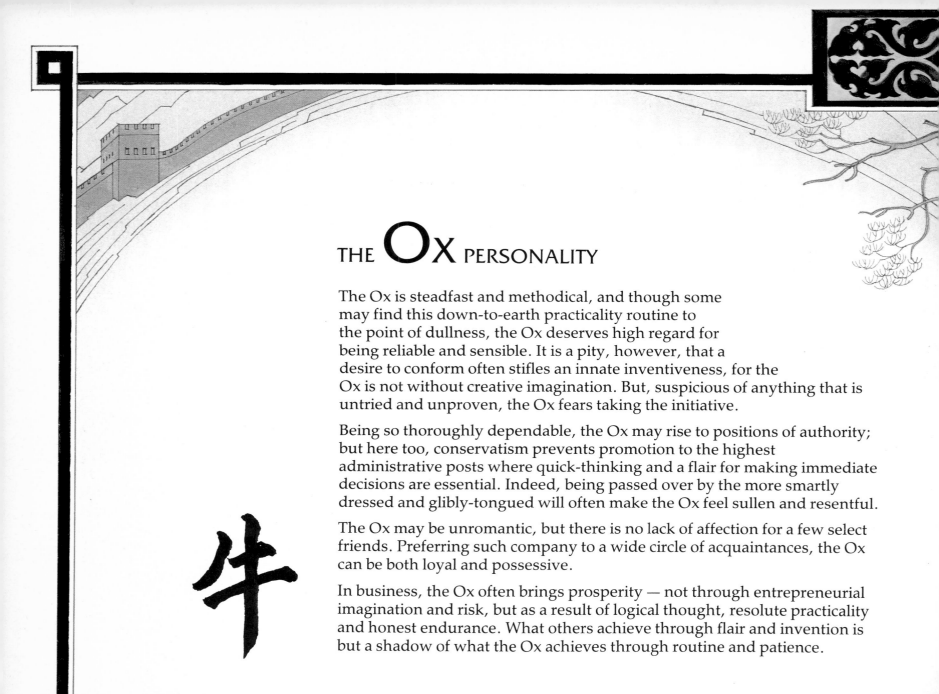

THE OX PERSONALITY

The Ox is steadfast and methodical, and though some may find this down-to-earth practicality routine to the point of dullness, the Ox deserves high regard for being reliable and sensible. It is a pity, however, that a desire to conform often stifles an innate inventiveness, for the Ox is not without creative imagination. But, suspicious of anything that is untried and unproven, the Ox fears taking the initiative.

Being so thoroughly dependable, the Ox may rise to positions of authority; but here too, conservatism prevents promotion to the highest administrative posts where quick-thinking and a flair for making immediate decisions are essential. Indeed, being passed over by the more smartly dressed and glibly-tongued will often make the Ox feel sullen and resentful.

The Ox may be unromantic, but there is no lack of affection for a few select friends. Preferring such company to a wide circle of acquaintances, the Ox can be both loyal and possessive.

In business, the Ox often brings prosperity — not through entrepreneurial imagination and risk, but as a result of logical thought, resolute practicality and honest endurance. What others achieve through flair and invention is but a shadow of what the Ox achieves through routine and patience.

THE SYMBOLISM OF THE OX 牛

The Ox has a prime place in Chinese astrological symbolism, and in fact appears on the first page of every Chinese Almanac where it portends the prospects of the coming harvest. Emblematic of agriculture in general, the sturdy Ox is also a symbol of diligence, perseverance, tenacity and thoroughness.

By nothing more than a coincidence, the second sign of the Chinese animal cycle also has the same name as the second sign of the Western zodiac. There, however, all similarity ends. *Niu*, the Ox, is the name ascribed to the last month of the Chinese Year, corresponding approximately to January, while Taurus, the Bull, is the equivalent of May.

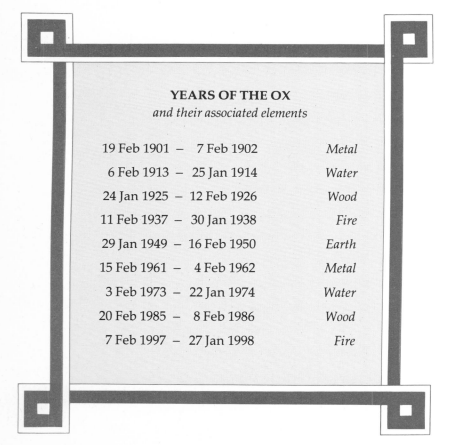

YEARS OF THE OX
and their associated elements

19 Feb 1901 – 7 Feb 1902		*Metal*
6 Feb 1913 – 25 Jan 1914		*Water*
24 Jan 1925 – 12 Feb 1926		*Wood*
11 Feb 1937 – 30 Jan 1938		*Fire*
29 Jan 1949 – 16 Feb 1950		*Earth*
15 Feb 1961 – 4 Feb 1962		*Metal*
3 Feb 1973 – 22 Jan 1974		*Water*
20 Feb 1985 – 8 Feb 1986		*Wood*
7 Feb 1997 – 27 Jan 1998		*Fire*

THE YEAR OF THE OX

This is essentially a time of stability, with the promise of steady expansion. Matters proceed happiest along established lines, and there may be little by way of innovation. But this does not mean that the year will be unfruitful; far from it. There are rich benefits to be harvested from the previous year's sowing, literally as well as metaphorically, since the Chinese associate the Ox with the earth, agriculture, tilling and ploughing.

But while established undertakings can proceed with confidence, it must be stressed that projects conceived during the Ox Year need a certain urgency.

In practical terms, this means that in business matters it is important to get that signature on the contract, whether yours or theirs, without delay. The opportune moment may pass all too soon. Or, if a marriage is contemplated, it would be unwise to consider a long engagement. The Ox is associated with bones, limbs, fractures, rheumatism and arthritis, and the Year of the Ox promises well for those suffering from ailments of this kind.

The ploughing of the earth also brings about the discovery of treasure. We might expect, therefore, some surprising archaeological finds during the Ox Year.

The Year of the Ox, like its associated winter season and pre-dawn hour, is a period of hibernation and sleep; and there are inevitably those who will be able to exploit whatever advantages this dormant period provides.

HOW EACH ANIMAL FARES
IN THE OX-YEAR

The Rat 鼠
The Rat and the Ox being astrologically compatible, this is a good year for the Rat-native. The Ox branch provides the receptive *Yin* quality which is dormant during the Rat's own *Yang* year. This presents longed-for opportunities to balance matters, and for getting affairs into perspective. Schemes which were put into operation during the Rat's own natal year can now be concluded successfully. It is not, however, a time to embark on new ventures unless there is every prospect of these being completed before the (Chinese) year is out.

The Ox 牛
This is the Ox-native's own year, providing an ideal time for slow and steady accumulation, and safe investments. There will be delays, but these will seem neither important nor irksome.

Stability is the key-note, with a great deal going on in the family, especially with regards to its increase, probably through marriage. Social life is to the fore this year.

The Tiger 虎

This is going to be a troublesome year, for the Ox is the one astrological sign of the Chinese cycle which clashes discordantly with the Tiger. Obstacles lead to frustrated plans, confrontations and delays. The best advice for the Tiger during an Ox year is to be patient, and to use diplomacy.

The Hare 兔

Those born in the year of the Hare will find this a pleasant, progressive year — not one of the best, but certainly not a time warranting complaint. Steady progress has a satisfactory outcome. It is a good year for family matters, and for socialising. If there is a choice between expenditure on holidays or home improvements, choose the latter course. Buying land is a possibility.

The Dragon 龍

Ancient astrological principles do not hold this year to be a good one for the Dragon-personality. For the artistic or creative Dragon, it will be a discouraging period, and a particularly bad one for the gambler and risk-taker, too. But routine work will bring its rewards. Problems at home, meanwhile, will have more to do with the fabric of the house than the people living in it. Security and insurance should not be neglected. On the positive side, travel is favourably aspected. Social life and romance play a significant role, but there is also a hint of scandal. Health is good.

The Snake 蛇

The Snake, unlike its *Yang* counterpart, the Dragon, can look forward to an excellent year. With all its signs in harmony, the Snake's financial acumen will come into its own in a year when everyone else is at a standstill. Now is the time to take advantage of every opportunity available, whether in business or romance. Step in quickly, and act while others are hesitating.

The Horse 馬

This is a better year for the cart-horse than the race-horse! For the Horse-native, the Year of the Ox is a plodding time; not exactly adverse, but slow and discouraging. But while there are few outstanding events this year, it is not a time for despondency. Concentrate on family life, and take encouragement from the fact that, next year, matters are going to be greatly improved.

The Sheep 羊

This is likely to be an uncomfortable year of retrenchment, with obstacles and misunderstandings at every turn. There are financial worries, and dangers to health from accidents, fractures, or chronic illness. The best advice for the Sheep during an Ox Year is to take things quietly. If the Sheep's expectations for this year are minimal, there is less likelihood of disappointment. There is, however, the chance of a windfall this year.

The Monkey 猴

The Monkey's natural exuberance is somewhat reined in the Ox Year, which might be a good thing for once. Travel is less important this year, and it is a better time to attend to matters, domestic or financial, which for far too long have been allowed to accumulate dust. Projects which were begun last year may be brought to a successful conclusion, but it is not the best time to embark on long-term plans. Social and personal life will be a little hectic.

The Rooster 鶏

After a particularly bad patch last year, the smooth running of the Ox Year is going to be understandably welcome. The Rooster's natural flair for showmanship will find plenty of opportunities this year, and opinions are going to be sought after, and listened to, with great interest, even respect. There are strong indications of travel or promotion, if not both. Altogether, a very fortunate year.

The Dog 犬

This is not the best of years for the Dog-native. Reversing the well-known image of the 'dog in the manger', this time it is the Ox which stands in the way of the Dog's ambitions, leading to resentment and ill-feeling. It is advisable to curtail expense this year, and to let ambitious schemes lie fallow for a while. There will be improvements in the following year, however, with eventual benefits accruing in the year after that.

The Pig 豬

This is a reasonable time for the person born in a Pig Year. Family life is certainly to the fore, and a change of home location seems to be indicated. But it will be advisable to seize all opportunities right now, since the following year is likely to be a disappointing one. Additions to the family, through marriage or a birth, are a strong possibility. This is definitely a much better year for women than for men. Some foreign travel is likely. Risky ventures should be avoided.

THE TIGER PERSONALITY

The Tiger is truly the embodiment of animal magnetism; a born leader, fiercely competitive, never afraid to fight. Not easily influenced, the Tiger's natural authority is seldom disputed.

The Tiger is also a great stimulant to others, either through brilliant conversation, where unexpected and novel ideas are constantly paraded, or by sheer physical presence, since appearance is often designed to overawe the less confident.

But while bravery, rashness and impetuosity are the hall-marks of the Tiger-personality, Tigers can nonetheless be warm, sincere, and even ardent in love. In this and other respects, the Tiger is unlikely to be restrained by convention. However, since the Tiger is essentially a symbol of masculinity and virility, the Chinese tend to distrust women born in the Tiger year, although doubtless the *Tigress*-personality would be to the fore of the Feminist Movement today.

The Tiger's competitive streak is excellent material for those business activities where aggression rather than diplomacy is likely to bring more favourable returns. Tigers are likely to succeed in sales, personnel management and uniformed careers. They should take care, however, that their manner does not gain them enemies along the way.

THE SYMBOLISM OF THE TIGER 虎

The Tiger figures prominently in Chinese folk-lore. His fierce strength can terrify evil spirits, and his picture was often pasted up on houses to frighten away the demons of disease, as well as on magistrates' courts to avert the spirits of corruption or injustice. Young boys were given tiger costumes and masks to wear, and dedicated to the Tiger god so that they would absorb his bravery. The luxurious coat of the Tiger is also associated with wealth; and Hsuan Tan, the God of Wealth, is sometimes depicted riding the beast.

The Tiger is indeed the King of Beasts for the Chinese, who have little first-hand experience of the lion, traditionally regarded as a vegetarian! (Even today, lion-dancers are given lettuces, to which encouraging sums of money are attached, as a reward for their services.)

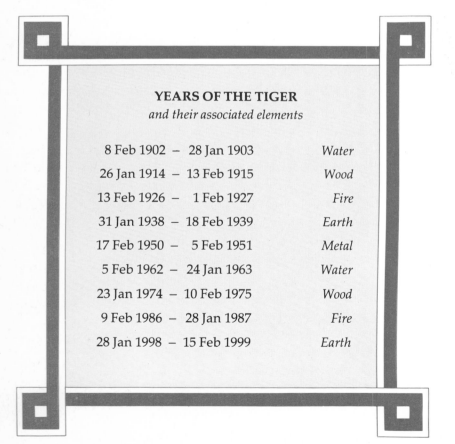

YEARS OF THE TIGER
and their associated elements

8 Feb 1902 – 28 Jan 1903	Water
26 Jan 1914 – 13 Feb 1915	Wood
13 Feb 1926 – 1 Feb 1927	Fire
31 Jan 1938 – 18 Feb 1939	Earth
17 Feb 1950 – 5 Feb 1951	Metal
5 Feb 1962 – 24 Jan 1963	Water
23 Jan 1974 – 10 Feb 1975	Wood
9 Feb 1986 – 28 Jan 1987	Fire
28 Jan 1998 – 15 Feb 1999	Earth

THE YEAR OF THE TIGER

Not surprisingly, perhaps, the Year of the Tiger is a time of dramatic and often dangerous change. For some, there will be success and adventure; for others disaster and calamity. Globally, it is a time of political upheaval: and certainly it is worth observing that both world wars erupted during Tiger Years. Even the weather cannot be trusted, with its promise of hurricanes and typhoons of unusual severity.

On a personal scale, it is a time of boldness and rashness, or even perhaps foolhardiness which may be mistaken for bravery. Here are the big stakes and the grand gestures. Time, therefore, for those planning vast and ambitious schemes to remember the Chinese proverb: 'He who rides a Tiger finds it hard to dismount.' For those under the protection of the Tiger, it will be a year of terrific progress, while others are sadly destined to be pushed to one side during this turbulent period.

In matters of health, it is a critical period, a time for taking the greatest care; and while the strength of the Tiger bodes well for the athlete, there is the ever-present danger of accidents.

Generally speaking, luck and chance are badly aspected during the Year of the Tiger. It does not bode well for speculative dealings or financial risks. Those who are keen on gambling are advised not to trust the favourites.

For the romantically-minded, the Year of the Tiger is the time for passionate affairs, when heart rules the head, and discretion and caution are thrown recklessly to the winds.

HOW EACH ANIMAL FARES IN THE TIGER-YEAR

The Rat 鼠
This is going to be a dramatic year for the Rat personality, bringing both despondency and elation. A great deal of activity is shown, and a considerable amount of travel indicated. But while the Tiger is harmonious with the Rat, benefits will only accrue to those who urge themselves forward. It would be unwise to sit back and hope for things to happen. Opportunities are there to be grasped by the determined.

The Ox 牛
Although the Ox and the Tiger appear to clash in the astrological chart, the Chinese say that 'one Ox can fight two Tigers.' The Ox, in effect, is the only Chinese astrological type who is able to overcome the adverse influences of the Tiger Year, and thus to withstand the temptation to overspend or to speculate unwisely.

But a struggle is there, certainly, as a continuous battle against circumstances or people may bring an endless succession of petty annoyances. The Ox is nevertheless able to come to terms with these difficulties eventually.

The Tiger 虎

This is the Tiger's ideal year; one of progress and achievement. Those born in the Year of the Tiger find fortune on their side, and can at last forge ahead, now that the restraints of the obstructive Ox Year have at last been thrown off. But there is a danger of over-enthusiasm and it must be remembered that this phase will not last. It would be wise to use the benefits of this year to make provision for leaner times ahead.

The Hare 兔

The Hare is the complementary sign to the Tiger — the *Yin* to the Tiger's *Yang*. Hares have much to look forward to just now, as their own prosperous year follows this one. Meanwhile, they can take the crumbs from the Tiger's table — in other words, while events may not seem to have a great deal of significance, there will be plenty of fringe benefits. Danger to friends will give the Hare much anxiety and possibly distress, since the Hare always feels somehow involved. Matters will sort themselves out by the end of the year, and it is a good time for inaugurating projects to be developed later.

The Dragon 龍

The Dragon and the Tiger are astrologically harmonious, which indicates a fortunate year. Now come those opportunities for advancement in business and romantic affairs, as well as reckless sprees. But there will be stern faces around as others find themselves having to face up to the realities of everyday life. The year also promises dangerous alliances. Dragon-types will realise their ambitions, but too late will find that the strings round the more attractive packages are very firmly tied.

The Snake 蛇

The Snake and Tiger do not form an auspicious alignment, making this a difficult year. All around, there will be activity and rush, and the Snake may well feel neglected. This is not necessarily a bad thing; there is nothing to be lost by a period of re-assessment. Indeed, during the present time, those who stand up in front of the crowd are more likely to receive brickbats than bouquets. Nor is it a good time to put forward new ideas; plans may go awry, and there are some who will be only too ready to find fault.

The Horse 馬

This is a good year for the Horse-personality, involving a great deal of socialising, leading to enhanced business prospects. If anything, the year is even better for men born under this sign than for women, although there is success in store for all Horse-natives. But it is important to remember that all this social activity is going to cost money: and entertaining, as well as the entertainment, are all going to make heavy demands on resources.

The Sheep 羊

For those born in the Year of the Sheep, this year coasts along in neutral. The Sheep-type has a complex personality, and may find that this year lacks direction. Many more decisions will have to be taken, and there is no use in turning to others for advice. The waywardness of the year is an adventure, however, and the rewards and the experience will be well worthwhile.

The Monkey 猴

During the Year of the Tiger, the *T'ai Sui*, or Year Marker, is in the opposing sector of the sky to the Monkey, creating a period of instability for those born under this sign. This may lead to depression or lethargy, but it is encouraging to think that this is only a temporary set-back. It will be better to stay on the sidelines and let others get on with their battles.

The Rooster 鷄

This is a middling year for those born in the Year of the Rooster, neither harmonising nor clashing with the Tiger. The time is ideal for planning new ventures, whether in business or romance, if long-term affairs are sought. Opportunities abound.

The Dog 犬

Good fortune attends the Dog all the way this year, and it is a happy time all round. Promotion is indicated, and business interests expand successfully. Dog personalities will have a more than usually active social life, and there are highlights in the romantic field. It is a good year for travel.

The Pig 豬

This is not an easy time for the home-loving Pig, who will find a state of turmoil all around. Problems are likely at home, either in personal relationships or with the actual fabric of the house. Expenditure could also be dangerously high, with unexpected calls on resources. So it would be unwise for the Pig to take on further responsibilities at present. But fortunately this difficult period is only temporary.

THE HARE PERSONALITY

The Hare craves company, and needs to belong to an established crowd. Safely within their social circle, Hares feel protected and secure; outside it, they are reserved and quite possibly withdrawn. However, even within the group, the Hare maintains a certain independence and, though hardly extrovert, can often become the focus of attention by being visibly on the edge of events. Thus, a gregarious and sociable disposition does not prevent the Hare from remaining aloof.

The typical Hare will be submissive, even humble, in a constant effort to avoid all confrontations. Happiest with friends, if somewhat inclined to gossip, this kind and benevolent lover of conversation, reading and literary pursuits may appear rather too meek but can be remarkably brave when faced with danger.

Traditionally associated with clear-sightedness, the Hare is an excellent judge of character, with an instinct for recognising sincerity in others and an almost uncanny ability for sensing falsehood. In personal relationships, even the most innocent deceptions will be identified almost at the moment they are perpetrated.

Another traditional belief accredits the Hare with the recipe for the divine elixir of life; and accordingly Hare personalities are often gifted healers, both of emotional and physical maladies.

THE SYMBOLISM OF THE HARE

Many strange legends surround the Hare, but none is more significant than the belief that this creature inhabits the moon, together with a three-legged toad, and that both have immortality. Because of its large, lustrous eyes, the Hare (or the Rabbit, for they are identical in the Chinese language) is associated with clear-sightedness and, partly thanks to this, the Hare is traditionally believed to possess the secret recipe for the elixir of life. (Ancient paintings depicting Paradise show the Moon Rabbit pounding away at a vat of magical herbs.)

Today, too, the Moon Rabbit remains one of the most popular characters with Chinese children, and he is feted at the Festival of Lanterns, on the fifteenth day of the eighth month, when the moon is at its most resplendent.

YEARS OF THE HARE
and their associated elements

29 Jan 1903 – 15 Feb 1904		*Water*
14 Feb 1915 – 2 Feb 1916		*Wood*
2 Feb 1927 – 22 Jan 1928		*Fire*
19 Feb 1939 – 7 Feb 1940		*Earth*
6 Feb 1951 – 26 Jan 1952		*Metal*
25 Jan 1963 – 12 Feb 1964		*Water*
11 Feb 1975 – 30 Jan 1976		*Wood*
29 Jan 1987 – 16 Feb 1988		*Fire*
16 Feb 1999 – 4 Feb 2000		*Earth*

IN THE YEAR OF THE HARE

Generally, this is a year for diplomacy and persuasion. It is certainly not the right moment for trying to barge ahead, since this will only result in sterile and time-consuming confrontation. On the other hand, it is an ideal time for dealings of a more agreed nature; the exchange of contracts, or the peaceful transfer of authority.

In the sphere of politics, this is not a year for dramatic change (all the revolutions having happened during the previous year — The Year of the Tiger). Rather, it is a period of increased awareness and concern for human rights, the underprivileged and the victims of unjust treatment. Internationally, much will be achieved to help those in need.

As the possessor of the recipe for the elixir of life, the Hare is credited with a knowledge of herbal remedies and medicine, and the Year of the Hare is seen as a suitable period for expansion in the field of pharmaceuticals or cosmetics, and dealings to do with herbs, drugs, or preparations of vegetable origin. Interest in alternative medicine will continue to expand.

Greater emphasis will be placed on the importance of family life, and there is good news for those wishing to expand their families this year; but those involved in illicit liaisons should ponder the Hare's procreative prowess.

With regards to health, this should prove to be a recuperative year; but beware the dangers of becoming dependent on medication.

HOW EACH ANIMAL FARES IN THE HARE-YEAR

The Rat 鼠
It will be a struggle to make progress during a year which is unlikely to bring the long-awaited break-through. Although it might have seemed, last year, that giant steps forward were finally being made, regretfully, the greatest asset any Rat could have this year is patience. In romantic matters, those born under the sign of the Rat may feel that their lot is not a happy one. Take great care with personal relationships.

The Ox 牛
This is a moderately good year for the Ox; the astrological aspects are well-established, and in all areas noticeable progress can be expected. In finance, there are moderate gains; while in romantic affairs, this is an exceptionally lucky period. With regards to health, conditions improve for those needing to take medicines.

The Tiger 虎

This is a curious year for the Tiger with apparently no major changes, but an undercurrent of activity, stimulated by some of the more outstanding events of the preceding Year of the Tiger. Following all that energy, movement and expansion, this is a year in which benefits will be seen in more secure finances, more stable personal relationships, and opportunities for physical and mental recreation.

The Hare 兔

This is the Hare's own year, and is thus the best of all for the Hare-personality. There is renewed vigour, greater confidence, and an improved outlook on life generally, putting the Hare in a very favourable position. A marked interest in the Hare is taken both by those in positions of authority and those whose aspirations are more romantically inclined. The year will be marked by an unusual number of happy family reunions. Generally, an excellent year.

The Dragon 龍

This is a moderate year for the Dragon, sandwiched as it is between all the excitement and activity of the Tiger Year which has just passed, and the frenetic rounds of the Dragon's own year, still to come. This fallow year, however, is a vital period of recuperation, even though to the Dragon it will seem routinely dull. The Dragon will have to be content with a time of stability, and dine out on last year's stories.

The Snake 蛇

The Snake, who so loves scandal, is this year uncomfortably close to being caught up in it. Dropping a customary mantle of caution, the Snake becomes involved in an incident which does not leave the reputation entirely unscathed. Canny as ever, however, the Snake is bound to make considerable social capital out of the affair. Finances are good this year; and those involved in the decorative arts, fashion, or cosmetics will make considerable headway.

The Horse 馬

The Horse will find this a year of effort; one of plodding rather than progression. Socially, it will be an active time; but in business, while there will be no shortage of work, little financial benefit will follow. In romance, several shallow, unfulfilling and brief encounters leave a feeling of dissatisfaction. In health, lassitude and depression probably indicate the need for a respite from the tedium of the moment.

The Sheep 羊

This is an excellent year for the Sheep, bringing success in many different forms, and helping to create an aura of accomplishment and general well-being. For career people, it will be a time of considerable achievement, and business matters proceed extremely satisfactorily. Those hoping to marry and settle down this year could choose no better time, although couples planning to wait before starting a family may find their schedules changed unexpectedly.

The Monkey 猴

This is a time of moderate progress for the Monkey. Activity generally will be restricted, with less social involvement and fewer practical enterprises. Financially, and romantically, too, the year is unremarkable. On the other hand, for those who work with ideas rather than with people or materials — the planners, programmers, and inventors — this is an excellent time for creative activity.

The Rooster 鷄

There have been better times for those born in the Year of the Rooster. A general feeling of frustration arises thanks to the fact that finances and opportunities are never available at the same time. Fortunately, this is only a passing phase: but during this inauspicious period, patience and caution are advised. It would be wisest to concentrate on the present position, perhaps making tentative explorations regarding future possibilities, instead of getting involved in albatross-like situations simply because nothing better presents itself at the moment. Patience will be a great asset.

The Dog 犬

Much of the impetus of last year carries over, and many projects begun then are brought to fulfilment. For those just setting out in marriage, the arrival of a new member of the family means considering the need to move house, and it would be wisest to do this during the current year.

The Pig 豬

This is a wonderful year for the Pig-personality. Family life is to the fore, and year is filled with joyful times together. There may be a move to a bigger house or better location. This would also be an ideal time to take a long vacation together. In business, the Pig has several successes, and the financial position improves considerably. Those involved in the arts, especially painting, can look forward to greater success.

THE DRAGON PERSONALITY

A lover of the exotic, the Dragon is one of the most flamboyantly extrovert characters of the Chinese astrological calendar. Elegant and with a good eye for spotting the latest trends, Dragon-types are always to the forefront of the fashion scene, ever ready to adapt what is *à la mode* to suit a very individual sense of style.

Blessed with an extraordinarily fertile imagination, the Dragon is forever dreaming up fresh schemes and ideas for new ventures, few of which are wholly practical. Such a mercurial character can be the despair of friends, and at work may even cause chaos if not surrounded by people capable of picking up the fragments of abandoned projects, albeit resentfully. Strong and decisive, resolute in a determination to follow interesting tracks which may lead nowhere, Dragons would become wealthy were it not for the fact that spectacular gains are as often as not offset by money wasted elsewhere.

The sign of the Dragon is an indication of an interest in the mysterious, the supernatural, and the occult. Dragon-types are also surrounded by an aura of good fortune which, however, disappears immediately a Hare approaches.

Dragons delight in any form of adulation, and both socially and in business they tend to seek out the bright lights. They are thus ideally suited to careers on the stage, but in general any sphere where there is close contact with the public provides a rewarding domain.

THE SYMBOLISM OF THE DRAGON

The Dragon is the only mythological animal among the twelve. This suggests some highly compelling reason for its inclusion; after all, it was a creature only known in imagination — or, as one cynic pointed out, had never formed an item of the Chinese diet.

The Dragon did indeed serve a vital purpose in the Chinese calendar. In ancient Chinese astronomy, one of the five most important constellations in the Heavens was called the Green Dragon of Spring, and its appearance used to mark the beginning of the spring rains. Thus the Dragon became associated with water and floods.

For the astrologers of ancient China, therefore, the Dragon, being associated with rain, was, far from being a malign creature, in fact the symbol of the life-force, eventually becoming the emblem of royalty, power and wealth.

YEARS OF THE DRAGON
and their associated elements

16 Feb 1904 – 3 Feb 1905	Wood
3 Feb 1916 – 22 Jan 1917	Fire
23 Jan 1928 – 9 Feb 1929	Earth
8 Feb 1940 – 26 Jan 1941	Metal
27 Jan 1952 – 13 Feb 1953	Water
13 Feb 1964 – 1 Feb 1965	Wood
31 Jan 1976 – 17 Feb 1977	Fire
17 Feb 1988 – 5 Feb 1989	Earth

THE YEAR OF THE DRAGON

Because it symbolises fertility, the Dragon is the sign of creation and innovation on a wide and expansive scale. In the Dragon Year, therefore, the time is ripe for bold strokes, wild, extravagant schemes, and dramatic, flamboyant gestures. Those involved in the arts, especially the theatre, can look forward to a period of increased attention to cultural activities. The time favours exchange visits, and festivals. The Dragon, being associated with astronomy, promises new discoveries in cosmology, too, which will excite great interest.

Politically, where the economy is sufficiently strong to bear the expense, large-scale, imaginative but controversial projects may be launched during the Year of the Dragon; while in areas where the economy is weak, there may be attempts to hazard everything on some enormous undertaking in the hope of financial recovery. Likewise, the Dragon symbolises the mystic and the occult, and general interest in these spheres will develop, with new sects or cults attracting great attention. Generally, this is not a time for the conventional; rather, those who succeed will be the rash or the eccentric. In business, bizarre schemes may prove to be more viable than expected. Indeed, the more fantastic the proposals put forward, the greater the chances of success.

The Dragon is associated with risk. Therefore, those involved in travel to exotic and isolated locations, or those whose occupations involve an element of danger, should not fail to take all necessary precautions to safeguard health.

HOW EACH ANIMAL FARES IN THE DRAGON-YEAR

The Rat 鼠

This is a period of great progress for people born in the Year of the Rat. The magical Dragon, symbolising royalty and wealth, brings about improved chances of promotion, expanding business interests, personal success, and a general prosperity which can be expected to last for about two years. It is an ideal time for experimenting and embarking on unusual adventures.

The Ox 牛

The Ox will have no time for the many bizarre suggestions and weird schemes put forward during the Year of the Dragon. Solidly practical, the Ox will dismiss such fanciful proposals as eminently unfeasible, and will seethe with indignation when authority, and years of experience, are by-passed in favour of some novel fad. Time will have to tell.

The Tiger 虎

An exciting year for the Tiger, who is able to push forward relentlessly, seeing successive struggles as challenges rather than obstacles. It is a period of risks, speculation and confrontation, out of which the Tiger emerges to a much stronger position. Health is generally good, although accidents are likely. In romantic matters, a tempestuous affair is a distinct possibility.

The Hare 兔

This year is full of pitfalls for the person born under the sign of the Hare. It is important to proceed with great caution, avoiding speculation and circumventing suspect ventures. As for business and romance, the wisest course is to keep to familiar paths. Children's illnesses may be a worry to the family.

The Dragon 龍

Who knows what outrageous schemes are likely to be proposed this year? For the Dragon-personality, this is a year of spectacular achievement and personal success, especially for those in the public eye or the field of entertainment. The romantically-inclined Dragon will have several opportunities to practise dalliance, while those who are more serious in their intentions may find that their ideal partner has at last entered the scene. Financially, an initially hectic period is followed by one of stability. In health matters, accidents are more likely than chronic illnesses.

The Snake 蛇

This is the beginning of an adventurous time for the Snake. There will be a temptation to over-reach oneself, but this is not absolutely the right moment for putting ambitious schemes into practice. Much can still be learnt from colleagues and associates. In business, the Snake-personality should stay in the background just now, studying trends very carefully. The ideal course of action is to observe, rather than to reveal.

The Horse 馬

Those born in the Year of the Horse will find this a stimulating year with the promise of foreign travel, and new and exciting projects. In business, the Horse will be offered a challenging position, and this may mean a change of situation. All kinds of novel prospects present themselves, and there will be a great temptation to speculate, not entirely successfully, in schemes of dubious merit. It is doubtful whether the Horse will remain entirely faithful this year, as it will be difficult to resist those opportunities which unexpectedly present themselves.

The Sheep 羊

Unfortunately, for those born in the Year of the Sheep, this may prove to be an uncomfortable year. Being shaken out of an established routine, and having to cope with all manner of innovative schemes is very much anathema. Those in business are likely to be confronted with unfamiliar legislation or technology; and at home, family life is likely to be disrupted, probably for some curious and unexpected reason. Personal relationships, however, should develop an interesting new dimension.

The Monkey 猴

This will prove to be a highly exciting year for the Monkey, with all kinds of opportunities to be explored. For once, the Monkey's skills and capabilities are acknowledged, leading to promotion and personal recognition. Those involved in manufacturing will see the successful launch of a new product. A new romantic association will be unexpected but sincere, and there is promise of a long partnership. Health is greatly improved this year. Travel is minimal.

The Rooster 鷄

This will be a very creative and constructive year for the Rooster, coming as a great improvement over the previous one. The influence of the Dragon adds stimulus, and there will be a general feeling that an onerous burden has been lifted. Confidence will be renewed, and personal relationships will blossom and prosper.

The Dog 犬

For those born in the Year of the Dog, the Year of the Dragon offers very little. Dog-personalities have to fend for themselves just now, as they contend with a seemingly endless number of obstacles. In matters of the heart, there may be a few tears; in finances, a few worries. But it is an ebb tide, not a drought; and happily, this difficult phase is a passing one. This year favours travel, especially over long distances.

The Pig 豬

This is a moderate period for those born in the Year of the Pig. Progress is steady, in business as in personal relationships; but a number of transient periods of excitement provide much to astonish and gossip over. These, however, will leave little that has a marked and lasting effect, and so time can be spent happily considering the addition of some unusual feature to the home. Cultural activities will be very rewarding.

THE SNAKE PERSONALITY

The Snake is the astrological companion to the Dragon; the *Yin* to the Dragon's *Yang*. However, while sharing many of the the Dragon's exotic qualities, the Snake is more restrained, and more refined; insinuating rather than extrovert. Indeed, in matters of taste and style, the Snake admires subtlety, preferring elegance of line to boldness of colour.

Snake personalities often make their way to the top, but they are by no means pushy, using others to get them there. They ensure that they are in the right place at the right time, which means when the right people are there as well.

Snake-types are also adept at giving the impression that they know far more about a subject than they intend to divulge; and while a strict sense of propriety prevents them from telling lies, they are not averse to double-dealing when it suits them. Fond of scandal, they are not above creating it, vicariously enjoying the frissons of others' disreputable behaviour.

The Snake's ability to gather up information suggests an aptitude for research, detection or academia, all areas which should satisfy the Snake's analytical brain. Social or domestic activities, meanwhile, will generally need to be tailored to allow for powerful sensuality.

THE SYMBOLISM OF THE SNAKE

The Snake, and its complementary sign, the Dragon, together form the House of Mystery; but whereas the Dragon is the gaudy magician, the Snake is the contemplative mystic. A correlative of this mysticism, however, is secrecy; and the Snake is closely associated with plots and counter-plots, scandal and corruption, the expression 'long snake' in Chinese meaning 'intrigue'.

On the more positive side, the Snake is regarded as the guardian of treasure. Indeed, some Chinese believe it to be unlucky to kill a snake which enters the house, as it could be the bringer of good fortune.

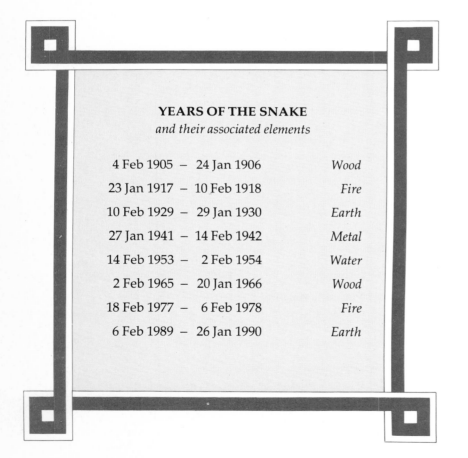

YEARS OF THE SNAKE
and their associated elements

4 Feb 1905 – 24 Jan 1906		*Wood*
23 Jan 1917 – 10 Feb 1918		*Fire*
10 Feb 1929 – 29 Jan 1930		*Earth*
27 Jan 1941 – 14 Feb 1942		*Metal*
14 Feb 1953 – 2 Feb 1954		*Water*
2 Feb 1965 – 20 Jan 1966		*Wood*
18 Feb 1977 – 6 Feb 1978		*Fire*
6 Feb 1989 – 26 Jan 1990		*Earth*

THE YEAR OF THE SNAKE

This is a time to re-consider the course of events which began in the previous and frenetic Dragon Year. It may mean that now one should back away from increasingly tense situations, and review schemes which may be on the point of running off course.

There will be back-biting and malice in the air, rather perversely due to the fact that this is generally a stable, calm and peaceful year, with congenital meddlers having little else to occupy them. In personal matters, it would certainly be unwise to engage in any kind of activity which would provide ammunition for purveyors of gossip.

The Year of the Snake is also a dangerous one for governments, who can be overthrown not only by revolution or the ballot box, but by the machinations of factions determined to embarrass those in power. But whatever political conspiracies there may be, the coming of the Snake Year is likely to indicate an improvement in the financial position.

Socially, the period is marked by an increased awareness of the needs of the environment: and a general war against the ravages of industrial encroachment on to the countryside will be matched in the cities by endeavours to improve the appearance of public places.

Generally, it is a time for refinement and artistic progress, revealed in fashion by a welcome trend towards grace, elegance, and economy of line, rather than the garish, startling polychromes which are often a feature of Dragon-style.

HOW EACH ANIMAL FARES IN THE SNAKE-YEAR

The Rat 鼠
This is a year of limited progress for those born in the Year of the Rat. Matters will proceed much more quietly during this year than in the last; and indeed, such advances as are achieved will be the results of careful planning in the past. It is important to continue to save this year, for leaner days ahead.

The Ox 牛
The Year of the Snake is a splendidly successful time for the usually staid Ox-type. There are opportunities for social advancement, bringing a wide variety of new friends and experiences: and business prospects are sound, with an additional sign of honour or recognition for an achievement in some other field. For those thinking of marriage, the time is very auspicious, with a likelihood of a younger partner.

The Tiger 虎

This year will not be easy for the Tiger-personality who is used to making headway without much opposition. Obstacles are likely to present themselves in the form of bureaucratic hindrances and legal tangles. Money may not be readily available, and there could be undue expense involving other people, perhaps through assisting members of the family, or an illicit affair which will prove costly. The year will not be without its anxieties, and health may suffer as a result. On the positive side, some unexpected financial gain is indicated.

The Hare 兔

This year augurs well for the naturally cautious Hare. Careful budgeting and an eye for value has ensured that the Hare has the resources to make some very shrewd business dealings. In personal relationships, however, the Hare is less careful and could well be the focus of gossip. However, the Hare cares not one whit.

The Dragon 龍

This year, many of the Dragon's more elaborate schemes and plans bear fruit, including those that were the object of derision when first mooted. The proof of considerable investments lies in their returns, which will vindicate the Dragon's faith in all such projects. While fully satisfying, the year will lack any great excitement, however.

The Snake 蛇

This is the peak time for people born in the Year of the Snake, when the stage is set for a grand entrance. The Snake's ambitions are not so much monetary or romantic, but personal status; and here, at last, comes the acclaim and recognition which has been elusive for so long. The Snake will be introduced to people of high standing, and those in the public eye will be accorded the most favourable criticism. Finances should be more stable than before, and business prospects are extremely sound. Career women will find this a very successful period.

The Horse 馬

This is only a moderate year for those born in the Year of the Horse, and progress may seem slow. It is a period of stability rather than expansion, allowing the Horse-type an opportunity to establish firm foundations for future dealings. There are no remarkably outstanding business prospects, and romantic affairs are marred by jealousy. On the positive side, the time is favourable for making improvements to the home.

The Sheep 羊

This is a happy year for the Sheep-personality; one in which events go well in all spheres of activity. Travelling with a group for a specific purpose, such as a research project or a convention, is likely, as is involvement in committee or voluntary work. Those involved in the arts, particularly music, will find this an extremely rewarding and creative period.

The Monkey 猴

The Monkey has to be particularly careful this year. Methods which have worked successfully in the past may have outlived their usefulness, and the Monkey could find formidable opposition in both business and romance. Financial deals fall below expectations, and an outsider may be given the promotion that had been expected. Personal relationships suffer, and an infidelity may lead to a break-up.

The Rooster 雞

For those born in the Year of the Rooster, this will prove to be an exceptionally successful year, since the Snake shares many of the Rooster's own preferences and priorities. Normally outgoing and forthright, the Rooster may decide to adopt many of the methods used by the Snake — discretion, tact, confidentiality — to make a considerable advance into the opposition's territory. Romantic affairs are highlighted this year, whilst finances are much more secure.

The Dog 犬

This is a moderate year for the Dog-personality, with the promise of financial security, but with a few worries still standing in the way. Fortunately, the position is becoming increasingly stable. Personal relationships jog along unremarkably. This would be an ideal period to start planning ahead, or to save for some ambitious project which can be put into effect next year. For the moment, however, large-scale projects are best left to one side.

The Pig 豬

Domestic bliss is rudely shaken this year by a number of unfortunate episodes. A previously close-knit family may suffer disruption due to certain members falling into disgrace, or being the target of gossip and scandal. This will not unnaturally cause great anxiety to any caring parents born in the Year of the Pig. Health, too, may be a source of worry, and it may be necessary to eat up some savings. However, the Pig — resilient and robust — will, as ever, cope with this.

THE HORSE PERSONALITY

It is acknowledged throughout the Far East that certain Years of the Horse may breed tyrants, revolutionaries and vandals with no greater desire than simply to charge forward. Thankfully, not everyone born in 1906 or 1966 will turn out to be an Attila or a Genghis; but collectively, those born in these years could prove formidable.

Whether male or female, Horse personalities feel more comfortable in the company of their own kind. The Horse may be afraid of the opposite sex, overawed by them, worship them, or disdain them, but relate to them — never.

Sporty and sociable, the Horse is the sort of person for whom clubs were invented. But sociability does not rule out competitiveness, although in sports the Horse prefers to be part of a team effort rather than perform as an individual. This is due in part to the importance which the Horse attaches to social standing. The Horse needs to feel successful, and to be seen as one of the gang.

Horse-types are good talkers, never short of conversation, though less quick with ready ideas. The latest news is always a good opening gambit, and the Horse is always keen to hear other people's opinions. Deep-seated prejudices, however, are hard to dislodge.

Love of social contact remains the most important force in the Horse's life; and whatever career is chosen, ideally it will involve close liaison with others.

THE SYMBOLISM OF THE HORSE

The Horse is one of three predominantly masculine signs in the Chinese zodiac, the others being the Tiger and, to a lesser degree, the Monkey. But whereas the Tiger symbolises the aggressive, martial side of human behaviour, the Horse represents those desires and wishes usually considered as characteristically male.

It cannot be by chance that Chinese astrologers of old deemed the Year of the Horse to have masculine attributes. The hour of the Horse falls at high noon; the month of the Horse is the one in which the Summer Solstice occurs: and at both these times, the sun, being the emblem of the *Yang* force, is at its maximum brightness.

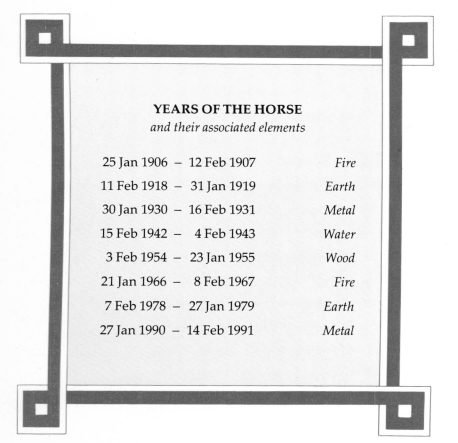

YEARS OF THE HORSE
and their associated elements

25 Jan 1906 – 12 Feb 1907	*Fire*
11 Feb 1918 – 31 Jan 1919	*Earth*
30 Jan 1930 – 16 Feb 1931	*Metal*
15 Feb 1942 – 4 Feb 1943	*Water*
3 Feb 1954 – 23 Jan 1955	*Wood*
21 Jan 1966 – 8 Feb 1967	*Fire*
7 Feb 1978 – 27 Jan 1979	*Earth*
27 Jan 1990 – 14 Feb 1991	*Metal*

THE YEAR OF THE HORSE

This is rarely a period of upheaval or dramatic change, and one should not look to this year for any shift in the world's balance of power. Rather, it indicates a strengthening of the present position, leading to greater political stability.

In the astrological chart, the Horse, significantly, is placed directly opposite the Rat. Accordingly, the Rat is the creator; the Horse, the consumer. The typical Year of the Horse is therefore marked by a considerable increase in business and commercial activity in the world markets. Particularly favoured are the men's clothing industry, athletics equipment, breweries, and sports car manufacture.

Less fortunately, the Year of the Horse also indicates waste, on a national scale signifying scandals arising from governmental maladministration. Personal and domestic spending should also be put into perspective at this time, to ensure that expenditure does not overreach the budget.

The robust Horse symbolises a sound constitution: and the Year of the Horse stimulates increased interest in outdoor pursuits and physical exercise. This is indeed a particularly good time to expect sporting records to be broken, since athletic activities figure very prominently.

Personal relationships may become exciting and even complicated during the Year of the Horse, but love — in the old-fashioned, romantic sense of the word — does not figure very prominently in what is basically a male-centred year.

HOW EACH ANIMAL FARES IN THE HORSE-YEAR

The Rat 鼠

During the Year of the Horse, the usually inventive Rat will find that new ideas do not find approval, and this may lead to frustration and a sense of being passed over. Life suddenly becomes highly competitive as the Rat struggles to keep pace with new-comers to the field. A tight rein must be kept on finances this year, while in personal relationships there is dissatisfaction with the present situation, and the Rat may look for a new partner.

The Ox 牛

Those born in the Year of the Ox are likely to suffer a few disappointments this year. The Ox-type is basically a tidy-minded person, happiest when things are ordered and methodical. The problems this year arise when carefully laid plans are disrupted by other people, and good work has to be started over again. Patience is one of the virtues of the Ox, fortunately, and diligence is amply repaid in the long run. A brief but temporarily serious romance is likely.

The Tiger 虎

This is an excellent period for those Tigers who are keen on sports and travel, as both are prominent in the Year of the Horse. Social activities are also very much to the fore, particularly during the summer. A renewed confidence and enthusiasm is rewarded by a management offer concerning a favourite project, especially for those whose work involves contact with the public. The Tiger's love-life, meanwhile, is likely to be very steamy.

The Hare 兔

This year will have both rewards and vexations for the Hare who is drawn into making new social contacts, either through business or a partner. The Hare-type normally enjoys meeting people, yet some of these activities may prove irksome, especially since they may lead to confrontation. They may be rewarding in unexpected ways, however. Generally, it is a stable year, although in certain areas progress may seem slower than usual. Romance is not without its heart-aches, but problems will eventually be resolved.

The Dragon 龍

Another bustling year for the effervescent Dragon in which personal ambitions are realised. If the Dragon-personality is involved in the performing arts, there may be many memorable moments. Life is very active socially, and considerable pleasure can be expected from the numerous contacts that are made. As usual, money will be spent profusely — but this year, rather more rationally. For once, the Dragon may decide to buy things which have a lasting value, rather than for their immediate appeal. Romance is tempestuous, and there is the possibility of the Dragon forming a lasting, but stormy relationship with someone from a completely different social set.

The Snake 蛇

The Snake personality may get into some awkward situations during the Year of the Horse. Progress is generally steady, but there are some unusual pitfalls. The problems this year, however, are really entirely due to the Snake's own doing, and are likely to be the result of attempts to meddle in other people's affairs. Business progresses satisfactorily, and finances are fairly secure. Plans for a romantic escapade, however, may backfire.

The Horse 馬

This is the Horse's own year, and the world can now be faced with renewed vigour. It is an excellent time for the Horse who wishes to travel; while, at home, any matters connected with the house — repairs or removals — can be attended to successfully. Luck generally is well-aspected this year; and, with finances being sound, speculation should bring worthwhile gains.

The Sheep 羊

The Sheep, being the complementary *Yin* sign to the Horse's *Yang*, fares well enough this year. There will be a welcomed opportunity to indulge in favourite pastimes and leisure pursuits: and if legal matters have been a problem, these will be favourably resolved. Romance has its good and bad moments.

The Monkey 猴

This could be a very successful year for the Monkey, if caution can be added to the customary inventiveness. Luck is high-lighted, and wins are likely through gambling or speculation, but these must not be allowed to cloud the Monkey's judgement. Travel is favourably aspected.

The Rooster 鶏

This is a particularly mixed year for those born in the Year of the Rooster. Family life will be uppermost with more than its usual share of events, some bringing happiness; others, anxieties. Personal relationships, unfortunately, are apt to suffer, and romance goes through a difficult phase. On the other hand, the year promises well for those involved in legal affairs, and matters concerning the buying of land are favourable.

The Dog 犬

The Dog and the Horse are stable companions; they work together, they play together, and so it is only to be expected that The Year of the Horse should be an especially good year for those born in the Year of the Dog. There is a very strong indication of travel either for a well-deserved vacation, or for business reasons, or even both, since commerce and leisure are each favourably aspected in the chart for this year.

The Pig 豬

The Year of the Horse progresses smoothly for those born in the Year of the Pig. There are minor problems, and a few pleasant surprises, but generally the year is one of stability. However, there is always some activity, if on a modest scale, and this does not leave the Pig much time for leisure.

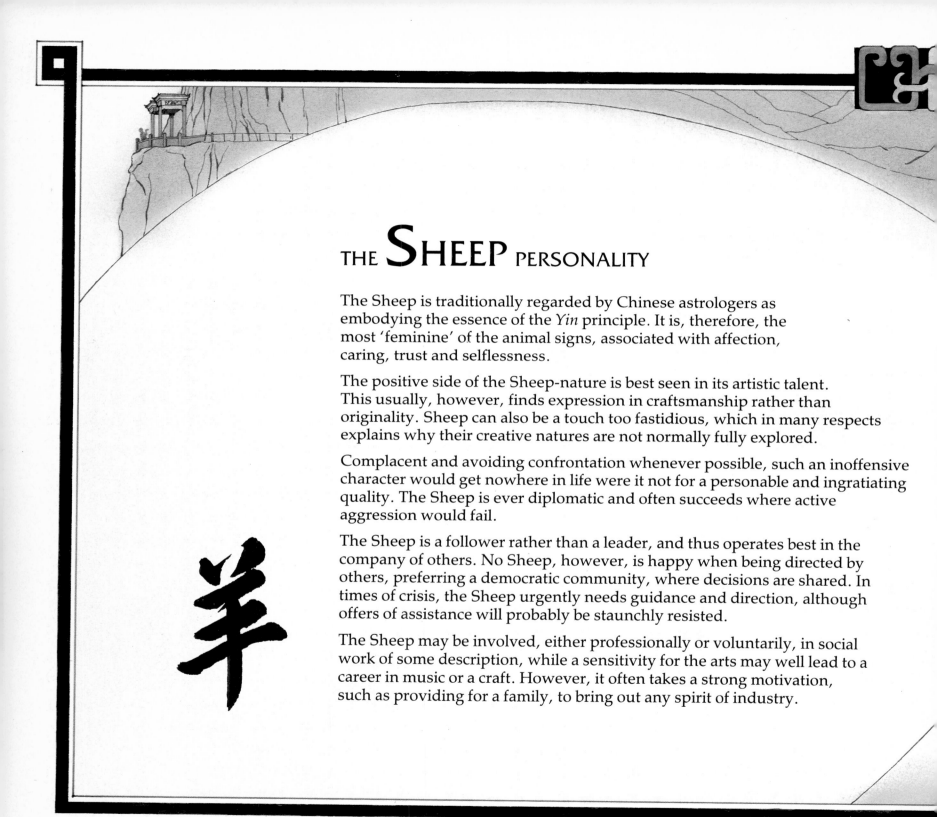

THE SHEEP PERSONALITY

The Sheep is traditionally regarded by Chinese astrologers as embodying the essence of the *Yin* principle. It is, therefore, the most 'feminine' of the animal signs, associated with affection, caring, trust and selflessness.

The positive side of the Sheep-nature is best seen in its artistic talent. This usually, however, finds expression in craftsmanship rather than originality. Sheep can also be a touch too fastidious, which in many respects explains why their creative natures are not normally fully explored.

Complacent and avoiding confrontation whenever possible, such an inoffensive character would get nowhere in life were it not for a personable and ingratiating quality. The Sheep is ever diplomatic and often succeeds where active aggression would fail.

The Sheep is a follower rather than a leader, and thus operates best in the company of others. No Sheep, however, is happy when being directed by others, preferring a democratic community, where decisions are shared. In times of crisis, the Sheep urgently needs guidance and direction, although offers of assistance will probably be staunchly resisted.

The Sheep may be involved, either professionally or voluntarily, in social work of some description, while a sensitivity for the arts may well lead to a career in music or a craft. However, it often takes a strong motivation, such as providing for a family, to bring out any spirit of industry.

THE SYMBOLISM OF THE SHEEP

The Sheep is the companion sign to the Horse, and together they comprise the House of Gender. The significance of this may need elaborating.

The roots of Chinese astrology go back to a social system and philosophy of three thousand years ago. At this time, dividing personality traits, modes of actions, careers, even actual objects and geographical locations into masculine and feminine categories seemed both logical and natural. While today such divisions are increasingly less applicable, and sports and athletics are no more the exclusive domain of the male, any more than meditation and poetry are the provenance of the female, in Chinese astrology such things are still seen in terms of *Yang* and *Yin*. These differences are symbolically characterised by the Horse and the Sheep in the House of Gender, and here all typically 'female' forms of behaviour are embodied by the Sheep, as 'male' forms are by the Horse.

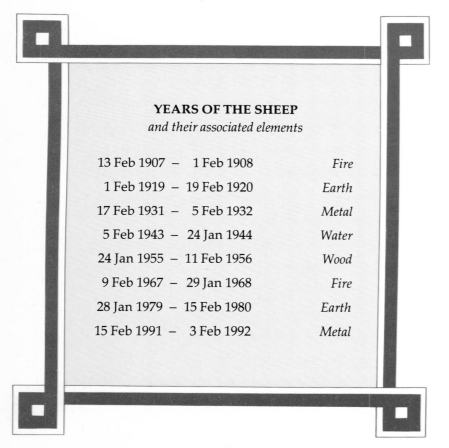

YEARS OF THE SHEEP
and their associated elements

13 Feb 1907 – 1 Feb 1908		*Fire*
1 Feb 1919 – 19 Feb 1920		*Earth*
17 Feb 1931 – 5 Feb 1932		*Metal*
5 Feb 1943 – 24 Jan 1944		*Water*
24 Jan 1955 – 11 Feb 1956		*Wood*
9 Feb 1967 – 29 Jan 1968		*Fire*
28 Jan 1979 – 15 Feb 1980		*Earth*
15 Feb 1991 – 3 Feb 1992		*Metal*

THE YEAR OF THE SHEEP

Whereas the Year of the Horse is marked by human achievement, the Year of the Sheep is marked by achievements *for* humanity, and new discoveries in medicine and surgery, the establishment of charitable foundations, humanitarian movements and all works which benefit mankind in some way will come to the fore.

The Sheep is essentially a consumer, rather than a producer — not of goods, however, but of ideas, suggesting that interpretation, as distinct from creation, of music and works of art will be favourably received. Thus, during the Year of the Sheep, a growth of interest in the performing arts greatly improves the position of those working in the fields of music and the theatre. In business, such things as fine art, precious stones, and *objets de vertu* will be regarded as healthy investments.

Politically, this is a period for reconciliation and arbitration. It is an opportune year to extend and strengthen diplomatic relations, and to reduce confrontation.

It is also the ideal time for those whose notions of true love are distilled from the very essence of romantic novels, for this year it is love, not sex, which plays the dominant role in matters of the heart. However, while personal attachments formed this year may prove to be enduring, the same may also be true of engagements!

Finally, this is a year when greater emphasis should be placed on the holistic approach to health. It is an ideal time to embark on a vegetarian diet, and to cut down on rich animal foods. Rest and tranquillity will pay dividends.

HOW EACH ANIMAL FARES
IN THE SHEEP-YEAR

The Rat 鼠

Life begins to show some improvement at last; and although ambitions may not be realised at present, it is at least encouraging to discover several avenues open for exploration. Progress may only be moderate, but the Rat is now able to come to terms with many of the difficulties that had seemed so daunting before, and a new experience enables problems to be approached much more constructively.

The Ox 牛

In the astrological chart for the Ox, the *T'ai Sui*, or Year Marker, is in direct opposition, indicating a time of obstacles and difficulties. Energies become dissipated, and efforts do not seem to bring the desired results. The main obstacles concern residence, not just the home itself, but also the locality. Monetary matters are very poorly aspected, and speculation or gambling should be avoided. On the bright side, romance and family life show up extremely well.

The Tiger 虎
Most people would be quite content with the quiet progress which this year has to offer, but those born in the Year of the Tiger are likely to find it rather slow, lacking the excitement and activity that they relish. Social life is without its usual glitter, and there are few new interesting faces to be seen. Luck, business prospects and romance are stable, however.

The Hare 兔
This is going to be one of the Hare's better years and there are several successes which bring with them renewed confidence. Whatever the Hare's ambitions regarding personal relationships, the outcome is highly satisfying. Social life seems to be associated with a widening of cultural pursuits, and there is an unexpected awakening of interest in fashion and personal appearance. Commercial activities are moderate.

The Dragon 龍
The usually exuberant personality of the Dragon may for once be stifled by hurtful criticism and petty-mindedness. There are obstacles in the way of projects which need to be finished; and fortunes are generally at an ebb. The Dragon should curb spending and speculation, as gambling losses feature very prominently in the chart. Travel is likely; and romance and health are both sound.

The Snake 蛇
Progress is good for the Snake-personality during the Year of the Sheep; and those whose professions are concerned with fashion, cosmetics, hairdressing and jewellery will find this an excellent year for business prospects, with expansion likely. But other commercial undertakings do not do so well, nor is it a good time to initiate new projects. Legal matters are successful, while established family relationships are happy.

The Horse 馬
The Sheep is the more meditative and reserved *Yin* sign to the active *Yang* Horse-personality. This may therefore soften those aggressive aspects of character which sometimes put the Horse at a disadvantage; and although this is the Sheep Year, the Horse

still stands to gain. In practical terms, it means observing and taking note of what more experienced people have to offer in the way of advice. Business prospects look very good, provided that the present course is maintained.

The Sheep 羊
For the Sheep, whose year this is, prospects are extremely encouraging. Social life improves tremendously; and as a result, romance is considerably heightened. At home, relationships are greatly improved, and there could be additions to the family. Any legal problems will be resolved to the satisfaction of all concerned and in business, matters run very smoothly.

The Monkey 猴
This is not a very harmonious year for the Monkey, and it will be tainted by confrontation for the pettiest of reasons. Business should do well, however, and there are opportunities for travel. But in several other areas, especially in personal relationships, there are difficulties.

The Rooster 鶏
This year is full of pleasant surprises for those born in the Year of the Rooster for, although the Sheep Year is generally regarded as a mild, meditative period — quite the reverse of what the flamboyant Rooster usually enjoys — a broadening spectrum of activites will bring the Rooster into contact with many new friends with a variety of unusual interests. Legal matters are satisfactorily concluded, while career ambitions have every chance of realisation now.

The Dog 犬
Those born in the Year of the Dog enter a period of conflict when the Year Marker, the *T'ai Sui*, enters the Sheep sector of the astrological chart. The home, which the Dog symbolically guards, is in danger, as is the area in which it stands. Expensive renovation and building repairs seem to threaten: but with the House of Expansion being the only sector which is favourably aspected, the answer may lie in moving altogether. Despite this, romance and family life show up well.

The Pig 豬
This is the happiest of years for the traditionally home-loving Pig; and love, romance, family life and personal relationships are all highlighted. Business may be slow, and general fortune only moderate; but with so much personal happiness around, the Pig is unlikely even to notice.

THE MONKEY PERSONALITY

An inventive and agile mind, together with an insatiable curiosity, produce a quick-witted schemer, always able to manoeuvre successfully round awkward situations. The Monkey is never at a loss for words, or ideas; but, alas, scruples are often in short supply.

Projecting an image of audacity and mischief, the Monkey hides a fundamental insecurity behind a mask of impudence.

Despite apparent popularity, the Monkey is never taken seriously, and this lack of recognition often leads to frustration. Since the Monkey detests being thwarted, resentment and pent-up anger can lead to bouts of depression. But once the Monkey learns how to deal with others on their own level — and it may take longer than expected to work this out — longed-for respect and approbation will follow.

Older and wiser Monkeys are able to channel their energetic and fertile imaginations into the solving of extremely complex problems; and such skills might be used by the micro-surgeon or the counterfeiter.

Generally, the Monkey is extremely versatile and can do well at almost anything. Success, however, can easily go to the Monkey's head, bringing out a latent arrogance which often alienates friends. But it is rarely long before the Monkey's agreeable humour and other engaging sociable qualities win them back again.

THE SYMBOLISM OF THE MONKEY 猴

The Monkey is one of the most popular and venerated characters of Chinese legend, and a significant proportion of the Chinese film industry today is dedicated to the dramatisation of innumerable stories concerning the Monkey's exploits.

The Monkey of legend had many innate skills, but only put them to good use when under the powerful restraint and skilful guidance of the Enlightened One. All the benefits of scientific invention may be put to darker purposes in the wrong hands, just as the techniques used to make weapons of destruction can be harnessed for good.

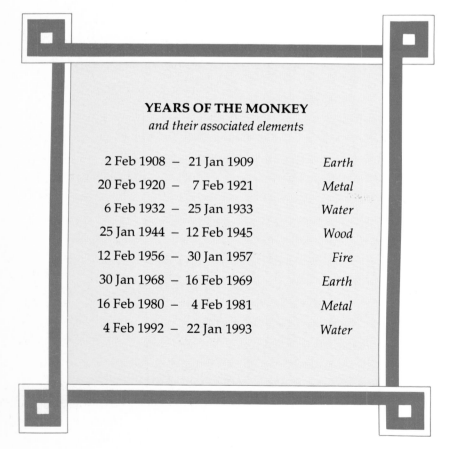

YEARS OF THE MONKEY
and their associated elements

2 Feb 1908 – 21 Jan 1909		Earth
20 Feb 1920 – 7 Feb 1921		Metal
6 Feb 1932 – 25 Jan 1933		Water
25 Jan 1944 – 12 Feb 1945		Wood
12 Feb 1956 – 30 Jan 1957		Fire
30 Jan 1968 – 16 Feb 1969		Earth
16 Feb 1980 – 4 Feb 1981		Metal
4 Feb 1992 – 22 Jan 1993		Water

THE YEAR OF THE MONKEY

This will be a year fraught with political squabbles, and one characterised by unstable government. Finances will be very shaky, and currency fluctuations will prove a headache for investors. In such a period of insecurity, it would be unwise to take speculative risks on a large scale; and although there are those who are destined to make a considerable profit out of the resulting chaos, their gain will be fortuitous rather than planned.

It is important to hold a strong rein during this shaky period, sound and firm management being an absolute necessity. It will be a great test of nerve, and those who survive will be in a much stronger position later.

For the romantically inclined, here is a year of confusion, mistaken goals, and restlessness. It will be best to let matters take their own course during this hectic year.

In matters of health, this is a period of peaks and troughs. Those who are normally extremely active, both physically and mentally, would be well advised to make sure that they allow themselves sufficient time to relax and unwind.

Although the negative side of the Year of the Monkey indicates mischief and trouble, positive features involve craft and dexterity. The field of science, particularly physics and technology, will see spectacular advances, and these have a marked and lasting effect. Skilled workers and technicians will be greatly in demand; and in one area at least, mechanical engineering, investment will be more secure.

HOW EACH ANIMAL FARES IN THE MONKEY-YEAR

The Rat 鼠
This is an excellent period, for whatever the Rat has been trying to achieve over the past few years is finally accomplished, and a long-standing ambition realised. Those hoping for examination success will have their hard work repaid handsomely: and in business, the lively and more confident Rat will find that prospects now look extremely healthy, with this present trend possibly leading to promotion. As a result of these developments, finances will be much more secure. But while social life again improves and romantic matters are much more satisfying, life at home may nevertheless have its awkward moments.

The Ox 牛
Those born in the Year of the Ox may find this a tedious year, with numerous irritations and petty obstacles in their path.

Ideally, it should be a period of quiet assimilation rather than activity. The best favoured spheres of action are study, short journeys, and agriculture or gardening. In romantic affairs, the need for a partner may be unfulfilled. Business, legal matters and family life fare only moderately, but speculations are slightly better than usual.

The Tiger 虎
This is likely to be a period of considerable friction for those born in the Year of the Tiger. Although financial and business affairs are generally very good, the signs are that the Tiger must face harrassment and delays. Family conflicts are likely, and some tolerance is needed at home.

The Hare 兔
Life does not seem to be taking the direction that the Hare would like just now, and a succession of unexpected events may cause unwelcome hindrance. The year is filled with minor vexations, and the need to deal with family problems allows less time for quiet and privacy. General fortune and official matters are poorly aspected; and finance and business fare only moderately. But romantic life is at a peak.

The Dragon 龍
Dragon-types exceed themselves this year. Having established a well-deserved reputation for eccentricity, they now, under the influence of the capricious Monkey, put their more extra-ordinary schemes into practice. Some of these wild ideas will pay handsome dividends. However, it is a pity that being buttressed by good fortune, the Dragon tends to be accordingly lavish, and very little is left at the end of the year.

The Snake 蛇
With several unfortunate aspects dominating the astrological chart, this is an awkward period for those born in the Year of the Snake. The House of Travel is very badly placed for long journeys, although shorter ones are favoured. Business is slow. On the other hand, cultural pursuits, romance, personal relationships and health are all well-aspected.

The Horse 馬
Since the presence of the Monkey benefits the Horse, a great improvement in conditions may be expected for the Horse-personality this year. Confidence increases, and general health certainly improves. As a result, relationships are strengthened, and renewed enthusiasm at work leads to a broadening of business interests. It is a very good period for innovation. The home is favourably aspected, suggesting an improvement in living standards, such as a move to a better house.

The Sheep 羊
Many minor difficulties present themselves in the coming year, and few things will fall into place. Prospects are poor for communication, and several problems arise as a result of mis-understandings, especially at home. Neither social nor business life is particularly outstanding; and personal relationships and romantic attachments deteriorate, which may lead to a degree of isolation. But for the Sheep who prefers to work alone, or for those following artistic pursuits, this will be a fruitful period.

The Monkey 猴
For those born in the Year of the Monkey, this is an exhilarating period; although it is not so fortunate for those with whom the Monkey comes into contact. Finances are sound, and tre-mendous strides forward are to be expected in business. Social life is very vigorous, but there are costs.

The Rooster 鷄
The Rooster is the complementary sign to the Monkey, and many of the better aspects of the year rule in the Rooster's favour. Career ambitions are realised, and business expands very satisfactorily. But though personal relationships and romantic attachments flourish, this is unfortunately not a good period for matters connected with the home.

The Dog 犬
This is a moderately good period for those born in the Year of the Dog, and the gains at the end of this year in material terms will be quite considerable. Improvements will have been made to the home, and social life will have been very busy indeed. But business will have taken up a lot of time; and, while ample recompense will have been made financially, personal life may suffer in some way.

The Pig 豬
This is not a good year for the Pig, with particularly bad aspects for those with home ties. In professional or lesiure activities, the fields of fine art, literature and music all promise success, as do horticulture and farming; but the Pig in trade or industry can expect a lean time. The gloomier aspects for this year, however, are adequately compensated by romance for those about to leave home for fresh pastures.

THE ROOSTER PERSONALITY

Although the Rooster is a male bird, astrologically this is a *Yin* or 'feminine' sign, the counterpart of the Monkey. Even so, the qualities it reveals — determination, pride, and confidence — apply equally to either sex.

Abrasive and bordering on the aggressive, the Rooster frequently alienates people who interpret frankness as rudeness, and style as affectation. These qualities, however, are the prerequisites for anyone as resolute as the Rooster in pursuing a career. A shrewd business sense will not prevent the Rooster from making seemingly extravagant gestures: but in fact there is usually an underlying motive not immediately apparent to the casual observer.

The Rooster is alert, joining a fundamental punctiliousness with precise attention to detail. The problems arrive when so many projects are taken on that, inevitably, the less troublesome get lost in the sheer volume. This happens, not just in business, but in personal relationships as well, when the quieter, more reserved members of the Rooster's social circle or family may be neglected or forgotten.

Stamina in business and vitality in play contribute to making the Rooster a stimulating companion — for those who can measure up to the mark. The Rooster has high ideals and, being a perfectionist, has little tolerance for people whose standards are second-rate.

THE SYMBOLISM OF THE ROOSTER 鷄

The Rooster is the *Yin* counterpart of the Monkey, and together they form the House of Career. Although this makes it a 'feminine' sign, the symbol of the Rooster is no misnomer and must have been chosen very carefully by early astrologers as an embodiment of direct, forceful and forthright behaviour.

Oddly enough, despite an association with the dawn, the Rooster presides over the evening hours. As such, it is a symbol of alertness, even at the time of repose.

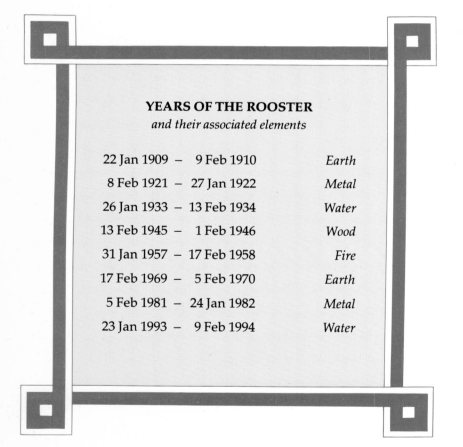

YEARS OF THE ROOSTER
and their associated elements

22 Jan 1909 – 9 Feb 1910		*Earth*
8 Feb 1921 – 27 Jan 1922		*Metal*
26 Jan 1933 – 13 Feb 1934		*Water*
13 Feb 1945 – 1 Feb 1946		*Wood*
31 Jan 1957 – 17 Feb 1958		*Fire*
17 Feb 1969 – 5 Feb 1970		*Earth*
5 Feb 1981 – 24 Jan 1982		*Metal*
23 Jan 1993 – 9 Feb 1994		*Water*

THE YEAR OF THE ROOSTER

For men as well as for women, this will be a year when career considerations take precedence over family and home matters. Since the Branch name for this astrological sign is *Yü*, for which the ancient Chinese character is a flask or bottle, during this year, viniculture, the manufacture and distribution of beverages, and by extension, the restaurant, hotel, and catering trades may be particularly favoured.

Other types of business which will do well during this year are those which involve the consumer directly — primarily clothes, cosmetics, jewellery, or anything designed to improve the appearance and well-being of the individual. Any dealings which take note of an increase of interest in fitness will also be successful.

In world affairs, a surge of passionate partisan or nationalist feeling can be expected, and minority groups who consider themselves subject to foreign domination may express their discontent forcefully.

The strength of individuality symbolised by the Rooster seems to augur badly for those hoping to establish romantic partnerships on an equal footing. It will be best to be prepared for sacrifices and disappointments.

In matters of health, prospects are ideal for those who can assert their determination to get well. It will be important this year to try and avoid being dependent on others; or, for that matter, on medication.

HOW EACH ANIMAL FARES IN THE ROOSTER-YEAR

The Rat 鼠
For those born in the Year of the Rat, this will be a strenuous time marked by several unwelcome events. But despite difficulties and set-backs, which may lead to a change of life-style, occupation or home, long-term results will be highly beneficial. Although there are losses, both financially and in personal relationships, there are also many significant, if unexpected, gains that emanate from this period of uncertainty.

The Ox 牛
Having emerged from a long, dormant period, and having kept very much to a routine for several years, the Ox now takes on a new lease of life. This is a year of spectacular change for the Ox-personality, and an excellent period for making a radical transformation, such as moving house or changing careers.

The Tiger 虎

This year seems to draw out all the Tiger's qualities. Steps forward are certainly made; promotion is likely, and business prospects are very encouraging. Luck and good fortune are on the Tiger's side, and travel is a strong possibility; while those involved in manufacturing or technology will gain financially. But many former friends could be alienated by the Tiger's ruthless hunger for success.

The Hare 兎

Those born in the Year of the Hare will find that this year has more than its usual share of irritations and hazards. The *T'ai Sui*, or Year Marker, is passing through the opposite sector to the Hare, blocking progress in such matters as commerce, social standing, and even romantic affairs. Patience is the only solution. Meanwhile, life does have its brighter moments. Outdoor and cultural pursuits will be very rewarding and family life will bring considerable happiness.

The Dragon 龍

Dragon-personalities are very much in control of their own destiny this year. The best aspects are those which concern the home, suggesting relocation. An unexpected financial gain could be followed by long-distance travel, and new proposals will find favour with those in authority. In business and commerce, there are several peaks and troughs. In matters of romance, personal life does not run smoothly either.

The Snake 蛇

This is an excellent time for those born in the Year of the Snake, although at first they may be a little disappointed to learn that it is principally home and family life which provide the greatest opportunities for happiness. All career and personal activities run very well, although in social life some paltry squabbles could lead to animosity later. Financially, this is not an outstanding year; but life is otherwise so enjoyable that this should prove of little importance.

The Horse 馬

The Horse-type will go through an irritable phase this year, discontented with those around and the things that they do. Much of this derives from the Horse's own conservative personality, for it will be a particularly forward-looking and thrusting time. Such a sense of dissatisfaction is bound to have an adverse effect on personal or social life, and may even taint business relationships, possibly creating a vicious circle of resentment. Matters which do not involve people proceed more favourably, and luck improves. Travel will be satisfying, and practical activities promise to be rewarding.

The Sheep 羊

A long period of inactivity at last draws to a close, and the Sheep-personality can start making plans for a new life. Family matters are finally settled to the satisfaction of everyone; and for those thinking about retirement, or perhaps considering a move to the country, no time could be better than the present. Recreational opportunities are highlighted, both for outdoor activities and quieter artistic pursuits.

The Monkey 猴

Career prospects for those born in the Year of the Monkey are as good as ever. The presence of the Rooster in the astrological chart benefits such areas as engineering, technology and building construction, while fashion and design are also fortunately aspected. Foreign travel will figure very prominently; but as there is little by way of chance or unexpected strokes of luck, speculation should be avoided.

The Rooster 鷄

In every respect, apart from romance, this is an excellent year for those born in the Year of the Rooster. Career activities move forward, and home and family life is both secure and rewarding. While the year may not be the best one for putting new ideas into practice, however, all goes superbly for the development of well-established projects.

The Dog 犬

The Year of the Rooster is an extraordinarily eventful one for the Dog-type, who will hurtle from one crisis to another. There are also some remarkably good strokes of fortune, however, interspersed with periods of personal conflict. Plans for improvements to the house, or relocation, for instance, cause clashes of opinion within the family. Business is only fair.

The Pig 豬

For the Pig-personality, finances remain steady; and social standing, both in public and private life, will improve considerably. At home, the family circle is well-knit, and worries about close relatives may be put to one side. Commercial dealings reveal only moderate successes, and high-risk speculations are not advisable. Personal and romantic life appears to be subject to stress.

THE DOG PERSONALITY

Fidelity, honesty and humour are among the predominant traits of a typical Dog-character. Such a likeable personality easily makes friends, usually long-lasting; and, being a steady worker, the Dog becomes a trusted and valued member of any community.

The Dog, however, is handicapped by conservatism, tolerating considerable hardship and inconvenience rather than choosing to make major changes. When circumstances force the issue, it takes a long time to adjust, no matter how improved conditions may be, and nothing is really ever as good as it was 'in the old days'.

Intensely defensive where friends and family are concerned, the Dog will not stand by while others are maligned: but sometimes a refusal to listen to warnings regarding the behaviour of children or other loved-ones can lead to severe domestic problems. The Dog has a sympathetic ear for other people's woes and is always ready with a shoulder to cry on. Rare displays of violent anger are almost always justified; but wrongs are quickly forgotten, and resentment only borne against those outside the intimate circle of family and friends.

Very active and liking sports of all kinds, the Dog can always be relied on to join in at social events, especially if these are outdoors. This can, however, lead to friction at home unless the partner is particularly understanding of the Dog's eagerness to mix.

THE SYMBOLISM OF THE DOG 犬

The Dog and the Pig together form the House of Family; but the Dog, being traditionally a protector and guardian of property, represents the fabric of the home, rather than the people in it.

In the Chinese astrological chart, the animal signs in closest relationship to the Dog are those of the Horse and the Tiger. While all three of these signs are overtly Yang or 'masculine', with the Tiger displaying aggression and the Horse ambition, the Dog reveals a more positive, constructive side and so symbolises guardianship and security.

YEARS OF THE DOG
and their associated elements

10 Feb 1910 –	29 Jan 1911	*Metal*
28 Jan 1922 –	15 Feb 1923	*Water*
14 Feb 1934 –	3 Feb 1935	*Wood*
2 Feb 1946 –	21 Jan 1947	*Fire*
18 Feb 1958 –	7 Feb 1959	*Earth*
6 Feb 1970 –	26 Jan 1971	*Metal*
25 Jan 1982 –	12 Feb 1983	*Water*
10 Feb 1994 –	30 Jan 1995	*Wood*

THE YEAR OF THE DOG

This year — the eleventh in the animal cycle — presents an inauspicious time for nations to consider attacking enemy territory, as resistance will be vigorous. The Dog, remember, is a sign of defence and protection. On the other hand, it is a favourable time to review and improve defence systems. At this time, governments would also wisely decide to increase the extent and powers of civil police to protect public order.

In business, the areas most likely to be profitable are those concerned with property and real estate, and preferably housing. Security services, and those providing defence equipment, are also in a favourable position.

In financial matters, it is particularly worthwhile checking securities and investments to see whether these need revising in the light of any recent market trends. The Dog is situated exactly opposite the Dragon in the astrological chart, which indicates unfortunate portents for speculation or high-risk ventures.

On a more domestic scale, it is a time to examine houses and buildings, and to see whether these afford adequate protection — not only against intruders but against inclement weather, too.

This is generally a favourable year for those concerned about their health, as the Dog symbolises inner-strength and fortitude.

For those with marriage in mind, now is an ideal time to settle down with one's partner. The Dog is the symbol of faithfulness and devotion; and the Chinese believe that marriages contracted this year will be happy and fortunate.

HOW EACH ANIMAL FARES IN THE DOG-YEAR

The Rat 鼠
In the Chinese astrological chart, the Dog and the Rat form a harmonious relationship. Consequently the Dog Year is a trouble-free time for the Rat. There is much to do creatively, especially if manual work or crafts are a strong point. Commerce and social life are both very active; but financially, it would be unwise to be too optimistic. There may be minor quarrels within the family, and legal questions arise. Romance does not appear in a prominent position.

The Ox 牛
The Ox bars the way of the Dog; thus, though the year may be beset with problems, the Ox forges on, irrespective of any obstacles. What might be serious set-backs for others are dismissed by the relentless Ox as insignificant. In the Year of the

Dog, the Dragon is the opposing sign, and land dealings — which normally come under the protection of the Ox — are now unfavourably aspected, possibly signifying waste. Commercial dealings are only fair, but for those hoping to marry, this year presents definite possibilities.

The Tiger 虎

The Dog Year presents excellent prospects for those born in the Year of the Tiger. Increased leisure involves foreign travel, sporting pursuits and a lively social life. For the businessman, especially the manufacturer, activity is also very pronounced. But personal life has its troubles.

The Hare 兔

For the Hare, this will not be a momentous year: but what it lacks in adventure is made up for in steadiness. Plans may be considered, but no decisions are taken at all. Business prospects are slow. Romantic activity is vigorous; and since that part of the astrological chart which rules the Hare's proverbial proclivities now approaches its zenith, this aspect of personal life, at least, can be regarded as favourable.

The Dragon 龍

The Dragon, which is the sign of luck, falls under the influence of the Dog this year, and it is thus a dangerous time for speculation. Attention should be paid to the home, since there may be adverse conditions there. Despite this, social and business life do extremely well, and there are opportunities for travel.

The Snake 蛇

Being the *Yin* counterpart of the *Yang* Dragon, the Snake must expect to suffer some of the adverse conditions which traverse the astrological chart this year. But fortunately, most of the malign influences seem simply to lessen favourable aspects, instead of creating additional hazards. Business may be slow, and social life lacks its usual velocity, but family life is cheerful.

The Horse 馬

Adventure beckons; and a year of exciting activity lies ahead as the Dog, the Tiger and the Horse now form a strong triangle in the astrological chart. For Horse sportsmen and women, this is an ideal record-breaking time. In business, the Horse will pursue deals aggressively, with highly profitable results. Because home and travel both stand very prominently in the present chart, moving house is also a strong possibility.

The Sheep 羊

The Year of the Dog is not kind to the Sheep-personality. Fierce competition can lead to unpleasant confrontations and, believing the struggle to be less than justified, the Sheep may leave the race for others to run. Instinctively, the Sheep is right, since two adverse influences dominate the chart at the moment. When both of these move away next year, the situation will improve considerably. Family life and opportunities for romance are much more rewarding, meanwhile.

The Monkey 猴

There are many surprises in store for the Monkey this year, and probably even more for the Monkey's acquaintances. As busy as ever, the Monkey will still find time to put some unusual plans into action; and although working or social partners may be astounded by some of the more brazen proposals, these nevertheless go ahead. Fortunately, luck is on the Monkey's side, or the schemes would end in total disaster.

The Rooster 鷄

The Rooster must regard the Year of the Dog as a time of challenge, otherwise a continuous succession of obstacles may be altogether disheartening. Fortunately, there are shoulders to cry on, particularly at home; and to judge by this year's chart, that is the best place to be. General good fortune is very badly aspected, and risks should be avoided. It is also wise to keep within the strict limits of the law, as minor legal wrangles appear. Avoid mixing romance with business, both of which are favourably aspected but at different sides of the chart.

The Dog 犬

Prospects are excellent in the Dog's own year. As protector of the home, the Dog may decide to move house or perhaps carry out significant improvements to present accommodation. In either case, the moment will be right, even if it is not possible to complete plans for another year. Social life and commercial opportunities are at their best.

The Pig 豬

Although it is not yet the Pig's own year, this year brings a foretaste of better times ahead. Now is the ideal moment to begin planning and saving for the big occasion, whether this is to be a world cruise, a better house, or an important social gathering. For although this year may be short of remarkable occurrences, the first inklings of some grand event will set activity in motion, and be the focus of attention for the latter part of the year.

THE PIG PERSONALITY

The last of the twelve astrological animals, the Pig is the symbol of conclusion and completion, too. Accordingly, the Pig's ambitions are concerned not so much with career, but the benefits which come at the end of it. While the Dog (the Pig's complementary sign) reminisces, the Pig looks forward to retirement.

Much more pleasant creatures than the Western use of the term would perhaps suggest, Pigs are home-lovers whose prime concern is the family. They are particularly natural beings, shunning displays or pretence, and enjoying company and jollity generally. Caring and industrious, Pigs are far from lazy; and their homes will bear ample evidence of an aptitude for carpentry, needlework, and other domestic skills.

In business, too, Pigs are the finishers, the ones who put the last necessary touches to a project, and in this respect they may become extremely successful financially. On the debit side, they are naive and trusting, falling easy prey to the confidence trickster. Pig personalities who opt for a career, as distinct from a job, enjoy such caring professions as nursing or counselling. Otherwise the Pig's genuine concern for others will become apparent through voluntary work and, locally, the Pig will almost certainly be known as a good neighbour.

Hard-working, hospitable and trusting, the Pig gets on well with most people, generally possessing a large and varied collection of friends. Inevitably some will take advantage; but though this may cause distress, the Pig will not wallow in self-pity nor harbour grudges.

THE SYMBOLISM OF THE PIG

THE YEAR OF THE PIG

The Pig is the name given to the last year in the twelve-animal cycle, and also signifies the last double-hour of the day, from 9pm to 11pm. Because it marks the close of the day, and the end of the cycle, it is associated with rest, peacefulness and satisfaction with what has been achieved.

It is fitting that, at the close of day, the most important place should be the home; and the most important people, the family. Thus the Pig symbolises the home in the House of Family. Indeed, in Chinese village life, the Pig was such an integral part of the home that the Chinese character for 'family' consists of the sign for a roof, under which is the character for a pig.

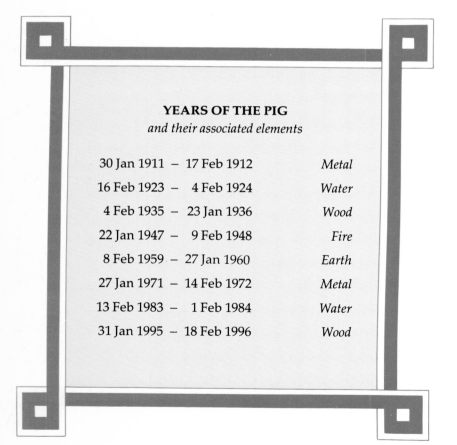

YEARS OF THE PIG
and their associated elements

30 Jan 1911 – 17 Feb 1912		*Metal*
16 Feb 1923 – 4 Feb 1924		*Water*
4 Feb 1935 – 23 Jan 1936		*Wood*
22 Jan 1947 – 9 Feb 1948		*Fire*
8 Feb 1959 – 27 Jan 1960		*Earth*
27 Jan 1971 – 14 Feb 1972		*Metal*
13 Feb 1983 – 1 Feb 1984		*Water*
31 Jan 1995 – 18 Feb 1996		*Wood*

When the sign of the Pig features prominently in a horoscope chart, it usually indicates a large family. Perhaps not unexpectedly, then, the Year of the Pig is considered to be the best year for dealing with family matters, and consequently an ideal period for arranging family gatherings and social events.

Since the Year of the Pig is the last of the cycle, it also signifies conclusion, and the closing phases of projects. Indeed, if matters which should have been concluded in the time of the Pig are left incomplete, then they may become almost impossible to finish.

Being the sign for the last hour of the day, too, and so signifying repose, the Pig indicates a dormant period. This may also indicate inactivity through insufficient use of latent abilities, or the need to let matters lie fallow for a while. In business, it signifies that the time is not suitable for expansion.

This is the right time for those who want to settle down and raise a large family. But those who are not so serious should make it clear that they are keeping their options open, or intentions could be misconstrued.

Internationally, it should be a peaceful period, with governments being more concerned with internal policies than foreign affairs. Larger powers, considering the withdrawal from occupied territories, will find that negotiations and treaties concluded during this period will result in a smooth and peaceful change of command.

HOW EACH ANIMAL FARES IN THE PIG-YEAR

The Rat 鼠

This is very much a transitional period for the Rat. Essentially the innovator, he finds that schemes which have been started now have to be finished, but outside help is no longer at hand. There is no problem in getting plans accepted, but finances are far from strong; and although there seems to be a great deal of enthusiasm, very little actually gets done. Social life is active, and romantic prospects become positive. Luck, however, is low in the chart, and speculative dealings should be avoided.

The Ox 牛

The Ox-type who is happy with the present situation will find this a favourable year. Dramatic changes are few, but the existing position improves considerably. There is a rise in status, either socially or professionally, and several personal gains may be made. General fortune and commercial activities are only modest, and travel does not play a great role; but despite this a number of successes are indicated.

The Tiger 虎
The Year of the Pig brings mixed blessings for the Tiger, with some improvements but several danger signals. In general, luck is on the Tiger's side, but there are problems. Commercial activities are fortunately aspected, and business matters can be expected to do well. Opportunities for speculation appear favourable. Legal matters, however, look extremely menacing with the threat of a law-suit. With regard to travel, danger signs are very prominent. Romantic matters are only fair, and there seem to be adverse conditions connected with the family.

The Hare 兔
Family life will occupy much of the Hare's attention this year, for the happiest of reasons. Those who marry at this time are destined to have large families, while those hoping to marry are likely to do so before too long. Those whose interests lie in the arts will be at their most creative, and musicians and artists can expect a wider appreciation of their work. Financially, however, the picture is less encouraging. Commerce fares only modestly; and as general fortunes are minimal, it is not such a good period for speculation.

The Dragon 龍
Fortunes gently rise and fall for Dragon-types this year. There is plenty of opportunity for social activity, but unfortunately there may be conflicts with acquaintances, trivial arguments and petty jealousies. This tends to mar romantic ambitions, and heart-ache is likely. Some decisions may be taken concerning improvements to the house; but as construction is unfavourable in the present chart, this should be borne in mind before making any irreversible decisions.

The Snake 蛇
There are many upheavals, conflicts, and upsets for the Snake this year, particularly in connection with the family, where some major problems arise. Several obstacles stand in the way of progress, and the Snake-personality seems destined to be impeded at every step. Legal action is badly aspected, and the Snake should avoid being drawn into law-suits. Manufacturing or technical trades are likely to suffer, and travel is not advised. On the positive side, artistic pursuits are favoured, and romantic activities are vigorous.

The Horse 馬
This will be a very moderate year for the Horse-personality, with few gains but little to worry about. New projects can go ahead as planned, bringing positive results in both business and social life. There are problems connected with the house, however, and expenditure on repairs or removals is likely.

The Sheep 羊
This year has excellent prospects for those born in the Year of the Sheep. The House of Family is very well placed, indicating — as one would expect — an increase in family membership, either through birth or marriage; and, likely as not, both. Frequent, short journeys are also prominent in the chart.

The Monkey 猴
There are several adverse conditions for the Monkey-personality this year. Ideas are received well, but the Monkey can get over-confident, and therefore careless. More positively, however, financial matters are in a healthy state; and for those in business, commercial transactions go well.

The Rooster 鷄
There is a marked improvement in the general conditions of the Rooster's life this year, after a long, dull period. At home, family relationships improve, with some old disputes reconciled, but there may be problems about accommodation. Career prospects are now much more firmly established, and this gives the Rooster greater self-confidence. Social events and romance figure prominently, but it is a pity that many former, worthwhile activities are accordingly neglected.

The Dog 犬
The Dog, being the companion sign to the Pig in the House of Family, will find this a happy year, with considerable activity at home. Matters do not always run entirely smoothly, however, and special attention may need to be given to children with emotional or health problems. There will be anxieties over travel. With commercial dealings moving rather slowly now, a stroke of good fortune will prove doubly welcome.

The Pig 豬
As the *T'ai Sui*, or Year Marker, moves into the final position on its twelve-year journey across the sky, it ushers in a momentary period of peace and tranquillity. Although foreign travel, excitement, and wealth do not figure highly, all Pig-types can expect a year marked by satisfaction and accomplishment.

There are three friendships which are advantageous, and
three which are injurious.

Friendships with the upright,
Friendships with the sincere,
Friendships with the observant,
These are advantageous.

Friendships with the conceited,
Friendships with the affected,
Friendships with the flattering,
These are injurious.

From *The Analects of Confucius*

RELATIONSHIPS

Will a Horse make a good marriage partner for the Hare? Will the Rooster work compatibly with a Rat? The pages that follow provide a guide to the nature of relationships between each of the twelve animal signs, with specific reference to interaction within the family, as well as in business.

RAT RELATIONSHIPS

with another Rat Rats have a high opinion of each other; and whether in love, friendship or business such mutual respect makes this a particularly successful team, providing that spheres of individual responsibility are clearly defined. The Rat-child may seem to be distant with the Rat-parent, but there is inner warmth.

with the Ox An excellent match in marriage and business, Rat and Ox complement each other very well indeed. The Ox-child, devoted and home-loving, is likely to stay with the family for longer than is usual.

with the Tiger Such a partnership is better for business than marriage; and if the latter, better that the wife is the Rat. The independent and forthright Tiger-child will be both a cause for anxiety and pride for the parental Rat.

with the Hare A Hare may cause heartache for the Rat in romantic relationships, and headaches in business partnerships, unless they learn to understand each other's needs. The Hare-child, meanwhile, is likely to take off without warning.

with the Dragon For the Rat, the Dragon brings stimulation and excitement in friendship, romance and business alike. The Dragon-child, too, will never cease to astonish the Rat.

with the Snake In marriage and business, the intellectually alert Snake is stimulating company for the Rat, always providing help and support when it is most needed. Relationships between Rat-parent and Snake-child of opposite sexes will be friendly, but there may be conflicts between mother and daughter, as well as father and son.

with the Horse Love must be very strong to bring together two people as different as this! Business partnerships are particularly likely to be fraught with differences. The Horse-child and Rat-parent, too, will experience difficulty in bridging the generation gap unless a conscious effort is made by each to accommodate the other's lifestyle.

with the Sheep Astrologically, this is not the finest match, but both partners are good at making the best of a situation. The Sheep-child, too, never seems to understand precisely what is expected by the Rat-parent.

with the Monkey This partnership is extremely harmonious, both in marriage and business. The Monkey-child will be talented but wayward, and needs both careful guidance and strong support on the part of the parental Rat.

with the Rooster Personal relationships will not be the most romantic, but otherwise, and particularly in business, each partner has valuable skills to offer. The Rooster-child will be devoted and loyal to the Rat-parent, but will tend to look elsewhere for emotional fulfilment.

with the Dog In business and romance, this partnership will outlast any difficulties. The Dog-child may go through a rebellious period, but in maturity will be a source of strength to the parental Rat. Friendships are likely to last for life.

with the Pig This is a happy partnership, where emotional needs are met, but working relationships could easily become too cosy. The Pig-child will need gentle encouragement when the time comes to leave the security of home-life with the parental Rat.

OX RELATIONSHIPS

with the Rat This will prove to be a happy partnership, in love and marriage, if the Ox is content to give the Rat a free rein. The Rat-child — intelligent and bright — will be a source of tremendous pride to the Ox.

with another Ox Socially, and in business, such partnerships will work, especially if there are others to keep things on the move. The Ox-child will work hard to fulfil expectations, and will bring great personal satisfaction to the parental Ox.

with the Tiger The attraction must be very strong here, for this is certainly not the easiest of partnerships, in romance or business. The Tiger-child will be a lively and boisterous member of the family, but may also cause the Ox some sleepless nights.

with the Hare A happy love-life is aspected, but one occasionally marred by jealousy. Business relationships, meanwhile, between the Ox and the Hare are much more successful. The Hare-child will bring great joy to the parental Ox.

with the Dragon It is easy to see the attraction that binds the Ox to the Dragon, but this is not an ideal relationship. Business partnerships are likely to work better if demarcation lines are thoroughly respected. The Dragon-child needs privacy; but given this, will return the Ox's affection.

with the Snake In romance, this is a curious partnership, but one that works. Disregard the scorn from outsiders. The business relationship is good, too. A Snake-child is likely to have an intellectual approach to the parental relationship, and there will be warmth and love, although this may not be overtly demonstrated.

with the Horse These obstinate partners may make life difficult for each other, but this is countered by a tenacity in love. In business, both Horse and Ox are well-equipped for confrontation; something best reserved for rivals than each other. The parental-Ox should also expect that the Horse-child will want to assert independence.

with the Sheep Though both Ox and Sheep share common interests, their views on life can be radically different, and at times this leads to conflict. There is no deep contact between Ox-parent and Sheep-child, who often find it difficult to communicate.

with the Monkey Socially, the Monkey is an entertaining partner for the Ox, providing an amusing relationship and also one where love can be sincere. They make for a good working business partnership, too. Although there are widely differing interests, the Monkey-child's impish nature will be very appealing to the Ox-parent.

with the Rooster The Rooster will provide vital stimulus to both romantic and working relationships for the Ox, and there is lasting harmony here. The Rooster-child will provide the Ox-parent with many pleasant surprises, too.

with the Dog A partnership between the Ox and the Dog, whether in romance or business, will always be under the shadow of mutual suspicion or insincerity. The Dog-child, meanwhile, may have difficulty in gaining the Ox-parent's confidence.

with the Pig This is a harmonious, but unadventurous partnership, well-suited to domestic bliss, or even for a docile working environment, but not particularly for high-powered business. The Pig-child will be warm and loving to the Ox-parent.

TIGER RELATIONSHIPS

with the Rat The Rat is likely to find the Tiger a domineering partner. Often, however, the relationship works, as this arrangement is usually satisfactory to both parties. Tiger-parents may be disappointed, however, that the Rat-child does not follow in their footsteps, but a closer relationship will develop with time.

with the Ox Never regarded as an astrologically favourable partner for the Tiger, in either romance or business, the Ox is not one to be manipulated. The Ox-child may at times appear wilful and disobedient to a Tiger-parent, but some indulgence does no harm.

with another Tiger Too much competition can make the Tiger-Tiger partnership fragile. Tiger-children will do great credit to Tiger-parents, and are likely to follow in their footsteps.

with the Hare This is an ideal relationship from the Tiger's point of view, particularly for marriage. Business partnerships work better when the Hare has a subordinate role. A Hare-child will bring the Tiger-parent great happiness, but little else.

with the Dragon This is a powerful partnership, both for business and romance. The Dragon-child will make the Tiger-parent very proud.

with the Snake This is an unlikely combination; and Snakes who team up with Tigers may have curious ulterior motives, since both in romantic and business situations there will be mistrust on both sides. The Snake-child may not relate to the Tiger-parent as readily as the Tiger would like.

with the Horse Here are two partners who recognise each other's worth, so that this is an ideal relationship for marriage, and a formidable one in business, where success is certain. The Horse-child will readily involve the Tiger-parent in friendships outside the family.

with the Sheep This relationship provides happiness in marriage and harmony in business: and a Sheep-child will be both affectionate and loyal to the Tiger-parent.

with the Monkey The most successful partnerships between Tiger and Monkey occur where both learn to recognise and overcome their mutual mistrust. The adventurous Monkey-child will need a great deal of guidance from the Tiger-parent, but will not respond to a heavy-handed attitude.

with the Rooster The strong physical attraction between the extrovert Rooster and the vital Tiger is not always enough to overcome their powerfully competitive instincts. The most comfortable relationship will therefore occur where both partners are able to retain a degree of independence. The Rooster-child will possibly leave home early in life, but despite this, remains affectionate to the Tiger-parent.

with the Dog An ideal traditional family life will follow a Tiger-Dog marriage; while in business, Dog and Tiger make a co-operative and successful team. The Dog child will share the Tiger-parent's enthusiasms willingly.

with the Pig The Pig is really not sufficiently sophisticated to hold the Tiger's romantic interest for long. In business, however, the Pig's ability to finish a job will benefit the Tiger, though here too there will be conflicts. The Pig child will probably always long for the Tiger-parent to provide a more settled home life.

HARE RELATIONSHIPS

with the Rat This is not always the happiest of partnerships, and whether in romance or business, the Rat should take care not to take advantage of the Hare, either emotionally or financially. The Rat-child may appear selfish, but the Hare-parent should avoid being over-sensitive.

with the Ox A romantic partnership will succeed better than a business one, unless financial success is not all-important. The Ox-child will prove extremely loyal and, in later life, very supportive to the parental Hare.

with the Tiger Ideally, this is a highly complementary partnership, wherein the Hare succeeds if the Tiger leads. In romance, and business, the Tiger is very supportive. Despite widely differing temperaments, the Hare-parent and Tiger-child will be very close.

with another Hare Friendships and family relationships are very strong between Hares. In business, however, material success is unlikely, unless there is involvement with another, more ambitious personality. The Hare-child will be very affectionate to the Hare-parent.

with the Dragon The Hare may be deeply attracted to the charismatic Dragon; but, alas, such feelings are not always mutual. In business and romance, there may be mistrust. The Dragon child's enterprise, meanwhile, will greatly impress the parental Hare.

with the Snake Chinese proverbs declare this to be the ideal marriage partnership. In business, however, be watchful. The Snake-child may appear cool and distant, but this is only due to an innate emotional reticence. In the Snake's heart, love is full.

with the Horse Although there is little common ground between the Hare and Horse, they will live and work together without conflict. However, personal relationships are likely to succeed better if the Horse-partner is the man. The Horse-child may be grown-up before the Hare-parent is ready to provide the key to the door.

with the Sheep A loving and truly warm relationship exists between the Hare and the Sheep. There is considerable mutual understanding in business partnerships, too; and the Hare-parent will find the Sheep-child both affectionate and sincere.

with the Monkey This partnership could bring heartbreaks unless the Hare learns to tolerate the Monkey's waywardness. In business, there is little mutual trust. The mischievous Monkey-child may bring problems, but there will be a strong bond.

with the Rooster The Hare finds the Rooster too abrasive, while the Rooster finds the Hare too casual. Such a relationship often works in business, where the personalities are complementary, but romantic attachments proceed with difficulty. The Rooster-child will be assertively independent but loyal to the parental Hare.

with the Dog This should be a stable partnership, both in marriage and business, but not without its moments of difficulty, although soundly based. In a large family, the quiet Dog-child may get overlooked; while a deeper parent-child understanding is likely to occur much later in life.

with the Pig A happy, natural relationship exists between Hare and Pig, especially in marriage, where family life is enviably secure. The Pig will prove a helpful, practical partner in business, too. The Pig-child will be a good friend and bring a great deal of extra comfort to the parental Hare's home.

DRAGON RELATIONSHIPS

with the Rat   Relations between Rat and Dragon types are very harmonious, leading to successful marriages and prosperous business partnerships. The artistic Rat-child is likely to fulfil the Dragon parent's latent ambitions.

with the Ox   The Ox and Dragon need to work hard together for an emotional relationship to last. In business, the Ox partner may be discontented. The Ox-child is unlikely to share the parental Dragon's interests, making close involvement difficult.

with the Tiger   This should be a very stable relationship for two individuals who recognise each other's talents. In business, the Tiger and Dragon make a high-flying team. But unless the Dragon-parent recognises the Tiger-child's individuality, conflicts may arise out of concern for the offspring's safety and well-being.

with the Hare   This is not the best of partnerships, as mutual understanding does not come easily. In business, particularly, confidence is lacking. The Hare-child, the Dragon-parent may find, will go his or her own way.

with another Dragon   Most remarkable is the dynamic business association and unpredictable personal relationship two Dragons inevitably make. The Dragon-child will certainly enjoy the Dragon-parent's lively company.

with the Snake   The Snake's cunning and the Dragon's flair are ideally suited to partnership, both in business and romance; and the parental Dragon will be pleased with the Snake-child's commonsense and logic.

with the Horse   A very sensible choice: the flamboyant Dragon needs to keep in touch with reality, and in business and love, the Horse proves a reliable partner. The Horse-child will be better organised than the Dragon-parent is ready to admit.

with the Sheep   This relationship is usually founded on infatuation, and a long-lasting partnership in business as well as romance will only be achieved with difficulty. The sensitive Sheep-child needs great understanding and attention on the part of the parental Dragon.

with the Monkey   A Monkey and a Dragon may seem to make an alarming partnership; but no matter how shallow they may appear to others, there is a deep mutual understanding. They also make a remarkable business team who should prosper. The gifted Monkey-child will be a good companion, having talents enough to match all the parental Dragon's flair.

with the Rooster   Not always an ideal relationship but these two exotic characters share many interests. In business, both benefit from each other's special qualities. The Rooster-child is likely to be assertively independent, as the Dragon-parent will find.

with the Dog   The Dog and Dragon are so opposite in nature that they actually complement each other. If they can pool their different skills and aptitudes, romantic and business partnerships could prosper, but both partners need to be able to lead individual lives. The Dog-child, however, may be secretly contemptuous of the Dragon-parent, and it will be important for the parental Dragon not to lose the child's respect.

with the Pig   The Pig will always bear the burden of the Dragon's waywardness, but will not necessarily be happy doing so. The Pig-child, too, may give more love than is received from the Dragon-parent.

SNAKE RELATIONSHIPS

with the Rat   In love, the relationship is likely to be happy, but mental rather than physical. A business partnership should also prosper. But the Rat-child will tend to reject the Snake-parent's advice, preferring to take an individual course of action.

with the Ox   In love, very much a 'lady and the gardener' relationship: truly passionate — but is it wise? A business relationship will be sounder, joining brain with brawn, quick-wittedness with practicality. The Ox-child will be very dependent on the Snake-parent's guidance.

with the Tiger   In romance, this is a very passionate relationship, but one which tends to blow over quickly. In business, extravagant ideas lead to financial difficulties. The Snake-parent may find the Tiger-child aggressive and difficult, but there is certainly no malice.

with the Hare   This is said to be the most successful of all romantic partnerships, and a business relationship should thrive, too. The Hare-child will also bring great happiness to the Snake-parent.

with the Dragon   This partnership is slightly better-suited for business than romance; and the Dragon-child will express many thoughts that the Snake-parent has often pondered.

with another Snake   Snakes find each other intellectually very gratifying, and in business and romance there are no problems here. A few extra outside interests and practical activities would make life more stimulating, however. The Snake-child will be a rewarding companion for the Snake-parent throughout life.

with the Horse   When there are differences in this relationship, they are usually not so much conflicts as misunderstandings; and partners tend to develop separate activities. The Horse child may have widely different interests from the parental Snake, and real communication occurs only occasionally.

with the Sheep   This pairing provides the foundation for a happy personal relationship and, in business, both partners work harmoniously. The Sheep-child will be affectionate, and should respond sympathetically to the moods of the parental Snake.

with the Monkey   After an initial enthusiasm, romantic attachments may have to undergo considerable testing; and business partnerships are likely to be subject to internal wrangles. The parental Snake will not always know what the independent Monkey-child is going to do next.

with the Rooster   Although proverbially ever at odds, the Rooster and Snake should in fact be able to form a lasting relationship, when the Rooster is not more concerned with career. Much more sound, however, is the business alliance, which promises great success. The Snake-parent will often find it necessary to help to put the Rooster-child's ambitious plans into practice.

with the Dog   If this relationship does not last, it will be the Snake's fault, for the Dog will remain a faithful admirer long after the liaison is broken. A business relationship should prove fair, too; but the Dog-child will require more affection than the Snake-parent is probably used to giving.

with the Pig   Although Pig and Snake are generally happy together, there is often something lacking, perhaps excitement, in this relationship. In business, the Pig-partner may not be completely involved. The Pig-child, meanwhile, will be loving, even when the Snake-parent is not.

HORSE RELATIONSHIPS

with the Rat Romantically, the chances are that this relationship will blow over, with the partners remaining friends. In business, a clinical, efficient working partnership exists. The Rat-child may appear disappointing in not following the Horse-parent's interests, however.

with the Ox Both Ox and Horse are rather set in their ways. Romantic attachments will therefore come slowly; but, once established, they last. In business, too, affairs are rather staid but altogether secure. The Ox-child will prove dependable and supportive to the Horse-parent.

with the Tiger This is an exciting choice of partner for the Horse. The Tiger will provide a jet-setting pace, romantically, and in business will help create a very sound and successful career. The Tiger-child will bring the Horse-parent great happiness.

with the Hare The Hare is not the best of romantic attachments for the Horse, who is subject to bouts of jealousy. In business, strife may also occur. A heavy-handed attitude towards the Hare-child will not improve a difficult situation, the Horse will find.

with the Dragon This relationship may provide an exotic life, but beware extravagance. The same stricture applies to business, where the Dragon-partner may have impractical ideas. The Horse-parent may be amused by the Dragon-child's ambitions, but will need to be openly supportive.

with the Snake The Snake and Horse have little in common to suggest a long-lasting relationship. The Snake hopes for a more intellectual edge to romantic attachments, while in business, there will be quibbling over details. The Snake-child may disappoint the parental Horse at first, but time will change this and lead to pride.

with another Horse This should be a very close-knit partnership, both in romance and in business, but unfortunately one which also tends to shut out other people. The Horse-child will be very close to the Horse-parent.

with the Sheep In romance, this is a very close attachment and in many ways an ideal partnership, despite many different interests. Horse and Sheep business partners achieve a good working arrangement; and the Sheep-child will be greatly loved by the Horse-parent.

with the Monkey Despite many differences, here is the basis for a long-lasting, if somewhat troubled relationship. Theirs is an unusual romantic attachment, since Horse and Monkey are more likely to be friends than lovers: but they do make an ideal two-person work team. Although the Monkey-child's interests may not follow the Horse-parent's own, they will nevertheless be respected.

with the Rooster This is one of the most successful partnerships. In a romantic situation, the Rooster may be more concerned with career; and in business, may take over the company. The Rooster-child will be very independent of the Horse-parent.

with the Dog This should be a very happy relationship in terms of romance, and should provide for a successful business partnership, too. The Dog-child will be loyal, friendly and supportive to the parental Horse, meanwhile.

with the Pig The Horse will be contented with the Pig's companionship, enjoying the pleasures of domestic bliss. A business relationship should proceed well, too, but may lack inspiration. The Pig-child will provide attentive care and comfort for the parental Horse.

SHEEP RELATIONSHIPS

with the Rat This is not one of the easiest of partnerships, with mutual mistrust, both in romance and business relationships. The Rat-child will be very independent of the parental Sheep.

with the Ox Ox and Sheep-types have many interests in common, so that conflicts over trivialities should not be allowed to mar both romantic and business partnerships. The Ox-child may appear truculent at times; but the Sheep-parent should learn to tolerate this and will find thereby a surprisingly worthwhile relationship.

with the Tiger In romance and business alike, this relationship will work if the Sheep does not mind taking a subordinate role. The Tiger-child will bring the parental Sheep cause for great rejoicing and comfort, too, in later life.

with the Hare A happy, loving relationship makes this an ideal marriage. Business partnerships are harmonious, too, but lack flair. The Hare-child will also bring joy and satisfaction to the parental Sheep, and family life will be very close-knit.

with the Dragon In matters of romance, the attraction of the flamboyant Dragon is understandable, but there could be many heartbreaks. In business, meanwhile, there is strife. The Dragon-child will be very different from the Sheep-parent, in all aspects of life, but nevertheless a cause for pride.

with the Snake The elegant but prudent Snake will bring glitter without extravagance, and both romantic and business relationships show success. The Snake-child will prove to be an affectionate prodigy of the parental Sheep.

with the Horse This is an ideal partnership which, whether in romance or business, is secure, fulfilling and built to last. There will be a close and warm understanding between the Horse-child and his or her Sheep-parent.

with another Sheep This is a partnership of like minds, and will prove successful in love, and smooth-running in business. The Sheep-child may become the Sheep-parent's favourite.

with the Monkey This is a curious partnership, in which understanding does not come naturally. A romantic attachment, however, may work — and a business venture more so — if the partners allow each other freedom to act independently. The Monkey-child will be self-contained and seem rather private to the Sheep.

with the Rooster In romance, the Rooster brings excitement and stimulation into the placid, domestic existence of the Sheep. In business, too, the Rooster may be very much the front-of-house partner; and in friendships, the Rooster will usually take the lead, too. The Sheep-parent will be very proud of the Rooster-child.

with the Dog In any relationship, romantic or business, the Dog-type tends to dominate the Sheep, who struggles to contend with this. The young Dog-child may seem precocious and overbearing, but will eventually become quieter and thus more gratifying company for the parental Sheep.

with the Pig This is a fine relationship for happy domestic bliss, and for partners in small, old-fashioned businesses. The Pig-child will be gentle and caring towards the Sheep-parent, and there will be very strong family ties.

MONKEY RELATIONSHIPS

with the Rat This partnership works well both romantically, where each partner appreciates the other's qualities, and in business, where similar interests are supported with different skills. The Rat-child may seem reserved to the Monkey-parent, but the love and warmth is deep.

with the Ox Although a somewhat unexciting partner for the lively Monkey, the Ox nevertheless brings stability to the relationship. Business partnerships, especially, will be the better for this. The Ox-child is reliable, supportive and steady, and the Monkey-parent will often be grateful for younger support.

with the Tiger Too much passion in romance and too many obstacles in business make this a fragile relationship and one that should be handled carefully. The Tiger-child may also resent the Monkey-parent's concern, seeing it as interference.

with the Hare This is an unsteady partnership, where true understanding comes slowly. In romance, just as in business, there is some mistrust. The Hare-child may disappoint the parental Monkey, but this is only because they do not share each other's values.

with the Dragon Their love is strange, but deep. Friends may shake their heads, but what of it? In business, too, there is a combined exotic and flamboyant style which prospers; while the Dragon-child may manifest some of the parental Monkey's own lesser qualities.

with the Snake Such a partnership may be more difficult to get out of than it was to enter, since there may be resentment at the constraints of both personal and business attachments. The Snake-child may seem cool and aloof, but the parental Monkey should not forget that need for recognition is great.

with the Horse This relationship should develop into a lasting, loyal friendship, even after the initial romance has gone. In business, too, a sound partnership should ensue. The Monkey-parent should also find the Horse-child reliable and hard-working.

with the Sheep This should prove to be a relationship without strife, but also without real common interest, in both romance and business. The Sheep-child may appear distant, but affection for the Monkey-parent is definitely there.

with another Monkey If they think they are the perfect couple romantically, why bother what anyone else thinks? In business, however, they do need the added stability of another partner. And if the Monkey-child ends up in trouble, who is to blame but the Monkey-parent?

with the Rooster While affection may appear shallow, both Monkey and Rooster recognise each other's talents. A business partnership is likely to be in some unusual setting, perhaps the world of entertainment. The Monkey-parent and a Rooster-child will have tremendous fun together.

with the Dog Despite obvious differences, this relationship will succeed, the loyal Dog-partner being a needed help in times of trouble. The Dog-child will also be tremendously loving towards the parent-Monkey.

with the Pig There is bound to be strife in this partnership, since Pig and Monkey have such widely differing priorities. In love and business, the Monkey puts career first; the Pig, the home. The Pig-child will also need great love and attention from the parental Monkey.

ROOSTER RELATIONSHIPS

with the Rat The Rooster will probably want more excitement in romance than the Rat is ready to provide. In business, too, there may be many differences of opinion. The Rat-child will be independent, and perhaps even distant towards the parental Rooster.

with the Ox This relationship should prove lasting, even when romance disappears, forming what might be called a 'sensible arrangement'. Business prospects are very good; and the parental Rooster will greatly appreciate the Ox-child's steadiness and reliability.

with the Tiger There are too many conflicts of interest to make this a conventional relationship. Romance is tempestuous; business, uncomfortable. The Tiger-child should be nurtured carefully by the Rooster-parent. Great potential may otherwise go to waste.

with the Hare Initial physical attraction may not mean a permanent relationship. In business, meanwhile, each may resent the other's methods, although differing attitudes could prove complementary. The Hare-child may seem lazy and careless, but is nonetheless anxious to please the Rooster-parent.

with the Dragon These two exotic characters strike a respondent note romantically. In business, too, they are likely to respect each other's talents. The Dragon-child will never cease to mystify the parental Rooster.

with the Snake According to Chinese folk-lore, this relationship does not work in marriage. But in business, such partnerships are likely to do very well. The Snake-child will also bring praise to the Rooster-parent.

with the Horse Rooster and Horse have little in common, and a relationship, either in love or business, may therefore prove difficult to cement. The Horse-child is also likely to make his or her own way in life, independently of the Rooster-parent.

with the Sheep There is a great deal of love here, and it should be carefully nurtured. In business, the Sheep should also prove a worthy, hard-working partner for the Rooster. A Sheep-child will be very affectionate to the parental Rooster.

with the Monkey This is a curious but intriguing partnership, both in love and business, providing a few stormy moments, but generally a highly productive relationship. The Monkey-child should be handled with care by the Rooster-parent, or the promise of a brilliant career may be shattered.

with another Rooster Two Roosters can lead to confrontations, and each must afford the other a good deal of independence for a harmonious relationship to result in either love or business. The Rooster-parent should take care, however, not to let the Rooster-child go his or her own way too early in life.

with the Dog Romantically, there could be unhappiness here, unless the Rooster is able to keep career separate from home, while in business, the Dog may shirk responsibility. The Dog-child will, however, always be loyal and affectionate to the Rooster-parent.

with the Pig Both home and career are well-matched in this partnership, where each understands the other's point-of-view. The Pig-child will also be a great comfort to a Rooster-parent in later life.

DOG RELATIONSHIPS

with the Rat In personal matters and in business dealings, there are likely to be some conflicts, but this relationship is more than able to weather any storms. The Rat-child will bring his or her Dog-parent great joy.

with the Ox There are likely to be some difficulties here, with each partner finding the other obstructive. A degree of mutual indulgence would benefit all business and personal relationships. Be warned: the Ox-child may get sullen and obstinate if the Dog-parent tries to interfere too much.

with the Tiger This is an ideal partnership for a fun-loving couple, with many shared interests. In business, a good working arrangement also exists. The Dog-parent will be very proud of the Tiger-child.

with the Hare If this loving relationship is based mainly on physical attraction, what of it? Business partnerships, however, need a much firmer foundation. The Hare-child may find it difficult to communicate with the Dog-parent on important matters.

with the Dragon This is an awkward relationship since the Dog does not regard the Dragon's flamboyance sympathetically. In business, too, there is some mistrust. The Dog-parent may not fully appreciate the Dragon-child's ability, either.

with the Snake This is not the best of relationships, there being few affinities to indicate a lasting partnership. Business ventures are rarely certain, either. The parental Dog should also guard against misunderstanding the Snake-child's ambitions.

with the Horse This is by far the most ideal partnership for the Dog, with mutual understanding and shared pleasures. In business, this is also a strong team. The Horse-child will amply reward the parental Dog's kindness in time, too.

with the Sheep In romance, there will be tears; in business, conflict: and yet there is much for others to envy in this love-hate relationship. The Sheep-child may feel lost at home, meanwhile, unless the parent-Dog is ever attentive.

with the Monkey This waggish duo enjoy life to the full. Romantically, they make an engaging couple; and in business, their unconventional approach usually succeeds. The Monkey-child will be very active, and may seem excessively so to the Dog-parent. A love of mischief is the key-note in this relationship.

with the Rooster Proverbially this is a poor relationship, and indeed affection has to be very strong to bind these two together. In romance, there are misunderstandings; in business, mistrust. The Rooster-child is very independent, the Dog-parent will find.

with another Dog In love and business, Dog partners know each other inside out. The Dog-child will also be the closest to the Dog-parent in any family.

with the Pig This should be a safe, long-lasting, but unexciting relationship both in romance and business. One of the most ideal family relationships. The Pig-child will be affectionate, and also well-loved by the parental Dog.

PIG RELATIONSHIPS

with the Rat Although they have little in common, Rat- and Pig-partners fulfil each other's needs. In marriage, the younger partner is likely to be the bread-winner; and business partnerships are efficient and uncomplicated. The Rat-child, however, may find little in the parental Pig's home to hold the interest.

with the Ox In romance, this will be a stable and conventional relationship, ideal for those hoping to marry and raise a family. In business, the Ox makes a good working partner, too, for the Pig. The Ox-child, meanwhile, will be a source of great comfort to the parental Pig throughout life.

with the Tiger This relationship tends to be a stormy one, often leading to tears. In business partnerships, there is likely to be conflict, too; while the Tiger-child may well leave the parental Pig's home at a fairly early age.

with the Hare This is one of the happiest of relationships for those planning to raise a family, which may be larger than average. In business, there are many new opportunities for both parties, and the Hare-child will bring to the Pig-parent great joy.

with the Dragon This is not always the easiest of relationships. Romance may go through trying times; and in business, there may be difficult periods. The Dragon-child may even embarrass the parental Pig, who should try not to be over-protective.

with the Snake The Pig could get hurt in this relationship as differences in outlook may be concealed until too late. The Snake-child will be independent, and often appear restless to the parental Pig when at home.

with the Horse These partners are able to give each other mutual support, leading to a happy, steady relationship, particularly where the Horse is the male partner. In business, too, success is measured by security. The Horse-child will also be sturdy and reliable towards the parental Pig.

with the Sheep This is one of the happiest of relationships, providing a harmonious home-life. In business, too, there will always be genial agreement: and the Sheep-child will always be a credit to the Pig-parent.

with the Monkey Unfortunately, this is one of the relationships which proverbially ends in tears. There are too many conflicts of opinion, especially with regards to priorities. In business, demarcation lines will be important. The Pig-parent will be inclined to worry too much over the Monkey-child.

with the Rooster What could be a fragile relationship will weather the storm if opposing views regarding career and home life can be aired. In business, it is important to bring differences into the open, too. The Rooster-child will surprise the Pig-parent with unexpected talents.

with the Dog The Dog will prove a faithful partner, and home-life will be happy but unremarkable. As a consequence, life expectancy is longer. A solid, if uninspiring business partnership may exist; and the Dog-child will be home-loving and loyal towards the parental Pig.

with another Pig Utterly contented, these partners lead a blissful life. In business, problems can always be left until later. The Pig-child, meanwhile, will never be so happy as when at home with the Pig-parent.

What may appear to be a calamity often gives rise to
fortune.

From *Tao Teh Ching (The Classic of the Way of Virtue)*
Lao Tzu

PREPARING A HOROSCOPE

The drawing up and interpretation of a *Ming Shu* horoscope is an ancient art, involving complex calculations. Here, however, the process has been adapted in order to enable everyone to unravel the secrets of Chinese astrology still further.

Take a few sheets of paper and a pen or pencil, and read on...

The complexities of casting a Chinese horoscope are compounded for Westerners by the need to know the date of birth according to the somewhat cumbersome Chinese calendar. However, by sacrificing the convenience of an entry for every day of this century, and using conversion tables instead, the basic data needed to set up a Chinese horoscope has been made sufficiently compact to be included here.

The tables reproduced at the end of this section produce results in absolute concurrence with the almanacs published under the imprint of the former Imperial Board of Rites, as well as the new official calendars issued by the Chinese government. The prospect of using them may appear daunting at first glance; but by following the step-by-step instructions, especially prepared for this book, calculations become surprisingly easy. No technical knowledge or mathematical prowess is required, other than an ability to add and subtract simple numbers.

There are four straightforward stages to the compiling of a Chinese horoscope: conversion of your birth-date to the Chinese system, calculation of the Four Pillars, finding the predominant Elements and, finally, interpretation of the horoscope in order to ascertain what Fate has in store.

You will need a sheet of paper, preferably lined, for initial calculations. Head this 'Calculation Sheet'; and, at the top, write:

● The name of the *querent* (that is, the person whose horoscope is being cast)
● The querent's date of birth: day, month, and year
● The time of birth, if known (If this is not known, put 'noon', as on average this minimises any slight discrepancies which are, unfortunately, bound to occur when the time of birth is inaccurate.)

Adjustments to the Time and Date of Birth

Whether you were born in Sydney or San Francisco, local time holds good for the purposes of Chinese astrology and no adjustments for geographical location are necessary. However, if the time of birth falls between 11 pm and midnight, the date of birth should be adjusted to the following day, since the Chinese day in fact begins at 11 pm: and if day-light saving was in operation, then an appropriate deduction of one or two hours from the time of birth should be made. Note that, in some cases, these two steps may have the effect of cancelling each other out.

Now write the letters **A** to **L** in columns, as shown. You are now ready to begin your calculations.

CALCULATION SHEET

S. J. WELLS

23rd October 1952/3.20am

CALCULATION SHEET

S. J. WELLS

23rd October 1952/3.20am

A.	G.
B.	H.
C.	I.
D.	J.
E.	K.
F.	L.

Converting the Date

A   At **A**, write the *day of the month* of the date of birth. (As an example, we shall use a birth-date of 23rd October 1952, and time of 3.20 am. The day of the month is **23**, so **23** is written on the calculation sheet at **A**.)

B   Using Table 1 on page 83, find the code-number for the *month of birth*. Write this number at **B**. (The code-number for October, in our example, is **35**.)

C   Using Table II on page 83, find the code-number for the *year of birth*. Write this number at **C**. (The code-number for 1952 is **42**).

D   An adjustment has to be made for leap-years where necessary. If the querent was born in a leap-year on or after 1st March, write **1** at **D**. Otherwise put **0**. (Leap years are those which are divisible by 4; 1952 was, therefore, a leap-year, and so **1** is written at **D**.)

E   Add the figures at **A,B,C**, and **D**. If the total is **121** or more, subtract **120**. Write this figure at **E**. If the total is between **61** and **120**, inclusive, subtract **60**. Write this figure at **E**. (In our example, **A + B + C + D** is **23 + 35 + 42 + 1**. This totals **101**, so we have to subtract **60**, giving an answer of **41**.) The figure at **E** will be a vital factor later.

F   Refer to the figure at **E** and note the last digit. This represents the Stem of the day. Make a note of it at **F**, and write alongside it 'DAY-STEM'. (In the example, **E** is **41**; the last digit is **1**, and so the Day-Stem is **1**.)

G   Turn to Table III on page 83. This will show your cyclical number for the *time* of birth. Find the day-stem (**F**) in the left-hand column, and cross-refer in the table to the time of birth. Write this number at **G**. (In our example, the time of birth was given as 3.20 am. In the third column of Table III, alongside the day-stem **1**, we find the figure **3**. This figure for the cyclical number of the time of birth is entered at **G**.)

H   Turn to Table IV on page 84. This is the Chinese Calendar Chart. Find, in the left-hand column, the date of the Chinese New Year which comes *before* the querent's birth-date. At the far right-hand end of this row is given the cyclical number for the year. Write this number at **H**. (Continuing our example, 23rd October 1952 will be found in the Chinese year which began with 27th January 1952. The figure printed at the right-hand end of the row for this year is **29**, and so **29** is entered on to the calculation sheet at **H**.)

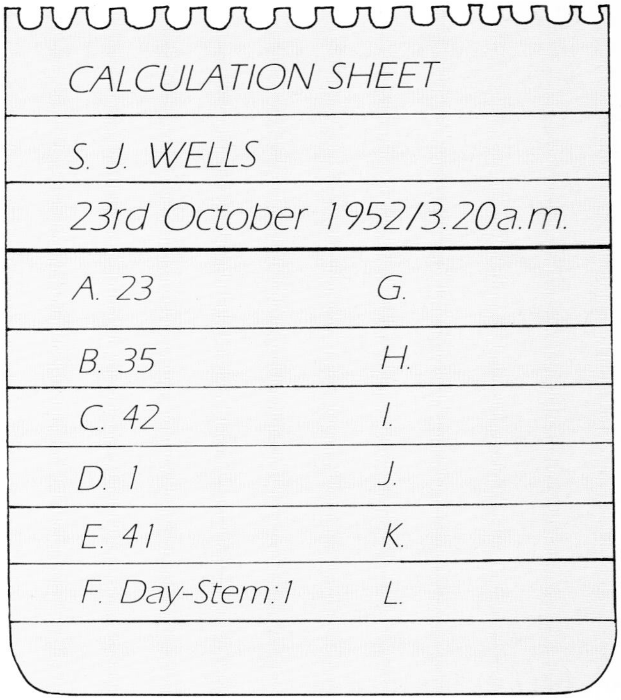

CALCULATION SHEET

S. J. WELLS

23rd October 1952/3.20a.m.

A. 23	G.
B. 35	H.
C. 42	I.
D. 1	J.
E. 41	K.
F. Day-Stem:1	L.

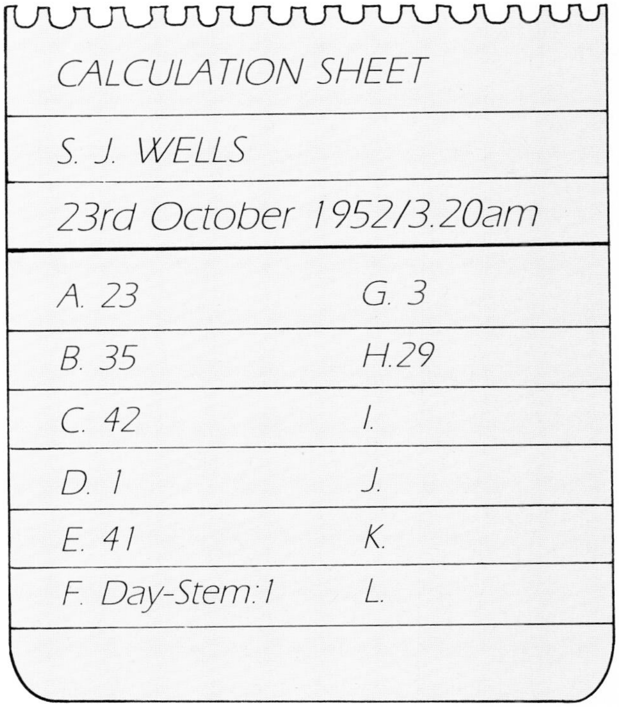

CALCULATION SHEET

S. J. WELLS

23rd October 1952/3.20am

A. 23	G. 3
B. 35	H.29
C. 42	I.
D. 1	J.
E. 41	K.
F. Day-Stem:1	L.

I While finding the cyclical number for the year, you will have noticed the year-type, giving both the animal-sign and Element for the year. Make a note of these at **I**. (From the calendar, we can see that 1952 was a **Water-Dragon** year.)

J To find in which Chinese month the querent was born, turn once again to the Chinese New Year date in Table IV on page 84, and look along the line until you reach the nearest date *before* the querent's date of birth. At the top of that column will be found the number of the Chinese *month*. Enter this at **J**. (Running along the line for the Water-Dragon year (1952), we see that the date immediately before 23rd October is 19th October which appears in the 9th month column. Therefore **9th month** should be written alongside **J**.)

K The next step, is to find the *day* of the Chinese month in which the querent was born. This is done simply by counting from the first day of the Chinese month (*see* step **J**) to the date in question. Enter this figure at **K**. (In our example, 19th October was the first day of the appropriate Chinese month. This would make the 23rd October the 5th day of the month. **5th day** is therefore written at **K**.)

Note that the Chinese *calendar* year is slightly shorter than the *solar* year; and to prevent the months from falling out of step with the seasons, certain months are doubled in length, so that they have 59 or 60 days. These 'intercalary' months occur seven times in every nineteen years, and the figure you enter at **K** could be as high as 60.

L Finally, we turn again to that crucial date, the first day of the Chinese month, which we first found in step **J**. Just below the date in the calendar chart is another code figure: the cyclical sign for the month. This is entered on the calculation sheet at **L**. (In our example, in Table IV on page 84, just under 19th October is the figure **47**, and therefore this is written alongside **L**.)

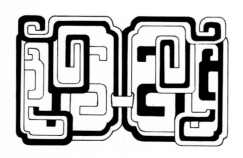

CALCULATION SHEET

S. J. WELLS

23rd October 1952/3.20am

A. 23	G. 3
B. 35	H. 29
C. 42	I. Water-Dragon
D. 1	J. 9th Month
E. 41	K. 5th Day
F. Day-Stem: 1	L. 47

All the calculations for finding the Chinese date, and the cyclical signs for the year, month, day and hour are now complete. We can therefore summarize the most important data as follows:

The Chinese Date: The **K** day, of the **J** month, in the **I** year. (In our example, the 5th day of the 9th month, in the Water-Dragon year.)

The Four Cyclical Signs:
The Hour —**G**
The Day — **E**
The Month — **L**
The Year —**H**

(In our example, **3**, **41**, **47** and **29**.)
You are now almost ready to start assembling an actual horoscope chart.

Setting up the Horoscope Chart

At the core of all Chinese horoscopes are the Four Pillars of Fate, and the Five Elements associated with them. The essential calculations being all but complete, it is now only necessary to turn to Table V on page 89 to compile the final data. This table short-cuts the complications involved in calculating the Elements associated with each of the Four Pillars, since — by using the four cyclical numbers which have just been established — all the information can be read directly from the one table.

You will probably want to put all the resultant information on to professional-looking charts, such as the ones shown on pages 92–95. (It is permissible to trace or photocopy these charts, provided that they are for your own immediate use only, and not otherwise published or used commercially.)

Now take another sheet of paper, and call this your 'Horoscope Notes'. On it, draw up a table as follows:

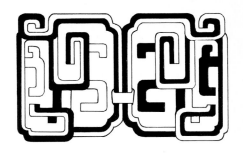

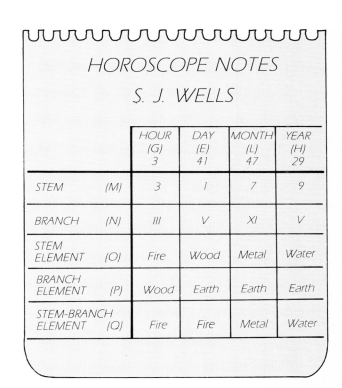

	HOUR (G,)	DAY (E)	MONTH (L)	YEAR (H)
STEM (M)				
BRANCH (N)				
STEM ELEMENT (O)				
BRANCH ELEMENT (P)				
STEM-BRANCH ELEMENT (Q)				

HOROSCOPE NOTES
S. J. WELLS

		HOUR (G) 3	DAY (E) 41	MONTH (L) 47	YEAR (H) 29
STEM	(M)	3	1	7	9
BRANCH	(N)	III	V	XI	V
STEM ELEMENT	(O)	Fire	Wood	Metal	Water
BRANCH ELEMENT	(P)	Wood	Earth	Earth	Earth
STEM-BRANCH ELEMENT	(Q)	Fire	Fire	Metal	Water

At the top of each column below the headings, write the four relevant cyclical numbers: that is, the figures at **G**, **E**, **L** and **H** on your calculation sheet. Now, turning to Table V on page 89, find the four appropriate cyclical numbers in the left-hand column. Reading across from these, you will be able to find the figure corresponding to the Stem (**M**), the numeral corresponding to the Branch (**N**), and the Elements for the Stem (**O**), Branch (**P**) and combined Stem-and-Branch (**Q**). Transfer all this information into the appropriate columns of your horoscope notes table as above.

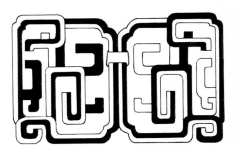

Interpreting the Birth-Date Chart

Having completed these columns, make a list of the Five Elements (Wood, Fire, Earth, Metal, Water), noting next to each the frequency with which it occurs in your horoscope notes.

Since there are twelve possible Element positions, but only five Elements, it follows that there can never be an exact balance of all the Elements in a birth-chart. Ratings of two or three, however, are ideal, as an even proportion of the Five Elements indicates a well-balanced and fruitful life.

```
WOOD            FIRE            EARTH
2                3               3
      WATER            METAL
        2                2
```

When there is a rating of less than two, it is usual for some other Element to have a very high, positive rating. Such imbalances can be countered, however, by striving to develop the recessive qualities of one's character; and if an Element is completely missing from a chart, it will be best to put this knowledge to positive effect by balancing the deficiency and associating, in either business or home life, with people whose own charts have a predominance of the missing factor. (It is worth pointing out that sometimes an Element appears to be missing from the chart simply because the date of birth either is not known, or else is inaccurate).

A rating of four shows where strengths lie, and where success is likely to be found. But, if a rating is above four, care must be taken not to allow this elemental quality to become overbearing for, if not channelled in a creative direction, this potential strength could turn instead into obsession, unyielding ambition, or self-indulgence.

It is important, too, to remember that during the passage of life, as the Elements progress through their natural order (Wood-Fire-Earth-Metal-Water), the Element of the moment may help (or hinder) development in different spheres of activity. Each year — indeed, each season, month, day, and hour — has its own cyclical sign, ruled by its particular element, which may harmonise or conflict with those in the horoscope chart. By drawing up basic horoscopes for critical dates and times, showing the Four Pillars and their related Elements, it is possible to compare these with your own chart, thereby seeing whether these are likely to be favourable times or not.

Elements of Personality

The following is a summary of the various personality traits associated with each of the Five Elements. Naturally, these differ depending on the prevalence of the particular Element in the birth-date chart. Accordingly, you will find details given for respectively low, medium, high and especially high ratings.

Wood (Creativity)
Rating of nought or one: conservative; neat; particular.
Rating of two or three: creative; artistic; literary; caring.
Rating of four: very creative; highly artistic; inventive.
Rating above four: highly imaginative; visionary; avant-garde.

Fire (Stimulation)
Rating of nought or one: equable; homely; quiet.
Rating of two or three: vigorous; spirited; active; stimulating.
Rating of four: charismatic; incisive; vital.
Rating above four: unrestrained; extravagant; vivacious.

Earth (Stability)
Rating of nought or one: flexible; rash.
Rating of two or three: reliable; trustworthy; practical.
Rating of four: highly practical; expansive; bold.
Rating above four: solid; circumspect; determined; obstinate.

Metal (Valour)
Rating of nought or one: gentle; generous; indecisive.
Rating of two or three: astute; competitive; sporting.
Rating of four: aggressively direct; enterprising; business-like.
Rating above four: entrepreneurial; competitive; unsentimental.

Water (Communication)
Rating of nought or one: secretive; shy; reserved; cautious.
Rating of two or three: intelligent; bright; talkative; lucid.
Rating of four: communicative; eloquent; adventurous.
Rating above four: loquacious; nomadic; intellectual.

Fortunate Stems

In your chart, you will find there are four different Stem figures at M. The ancient astrologers maintained that three particular combinations of these Stems (2–3–4, 1–5–7 and 8–9–10) are extremely fortunate. The presence of these groups of Stems in a chart indicates that the querent is destined to reach high office: and Stems which form regular groupings (such as 1–3–5, 2–4–6, and 1–4–7) are also harmonious, indicating success.

Other fortunate Stem pairs are 'opposites'. If the numbers 1 to 10 are written in a circle, then the pairs 1–6, 2–7, 3–8, 4–9 and 5–10 would be 'opposites'. Opposite Stems in the chart portend a particularly happy and peaceful life.

Harmonious Branches

Just as there are fortunate Stems, so certain combinations of Branches, represented by the numerals I to XII, are particularly auspicious. They can be found by writing out the numerals in a circle. Those Branches that then stand at twelve, four and eight o'clock to each other are extremely compatible, and Branches in a birth chart bearing this relationship reveal a remarkable degree of inner peace and tranquillity. Branches that are two hours apart are also favourable, suggesting a consistently contented spirit. One hour intervals are neither good nor bad, while those three hours apart tend towards adversity. Opposites — that is, Branches six hours apart — are decidedly dissonant and hint at inner conflict.

You have now compiled the basic horoscope for the date of birth: and from this, you should be able to form a general character assessment based on the animal of the year of birth. More detailed personality traits are revealed, in the chart, by the proportions of the Five Elements present. There is an art to this, which grows with experience and confidence. Meanwhile, all the information needed is contained in the present volume, and a polished efficiency can be gained with time and application.

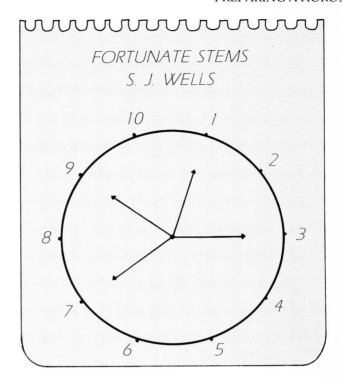

FORTUNATE STEMS
S. J. WELLS

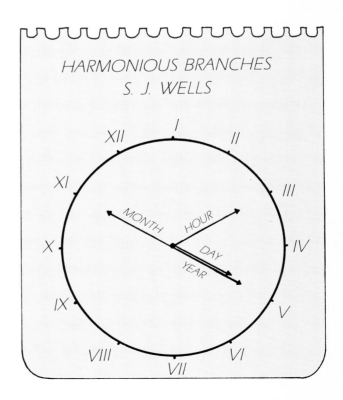

HARMONIOUS BRANCHES
S. J. WELLS

Charting the Life-Cycle

Finally, we come to what is certainly the most fascinating part of the Chinese horoscope: the setting up of a Chart which will map out the peaks and troughs of an individual's life.

According to Chinese astrology, the life span is divided into twelve distinctive phases, from conception to burial, known as the 'Life-Cycle Palaces'. These represent significant stages in life and career, and are as follows:

(VIII) Conception	(IX) Babyhood	(X) Infancy
(XI) Childhood	(XII) Adolescence	(I) *Kuan Tai*
(II) Adulthood	(III) Maturity	(IV) Retirement
(V) Decline	(VI) Final Years	(VIII) Burial

Note that, though *Kuan Tai* (Matriculation) occurs at about the age of twenty-one, it is recognised as the *first* of the Life-Cycle Palaces, representing the zenith of the horoscope chart.

The varying importance of the twelve stages in life depends on the impact of Five Forces known as *Fate, Seal, Official, Wealth,* and *Opportunity.* To find which Forces come to bear at different times in life, it is only necessary to make some simple calculations.

Turn to your horoscope notes and find the Element of the Branch of the Birth Year (**P/H**). This is the 'Element of Fate' (**R**). The Elements associated with the other Forces can readily be found by means of the table below.

If the Fate is in —	WOOD	FIRE	EARTH	METAL	WATER
the Seal is in —	Fire	Earth	Metal	Water	Wood
the Official is in —	Earth	Metal	Water	Wood	Fire
the Wealth is in —	Metal	Water	Wood	Fire	Earth
the Opportunity is in —	Water	Wood	Fire	Earth	Metal

Now, turning to your horoscope notes, find firstly the Branch of the Birth Month (**N/L**), and secondly the Stem of the Birth Year (**M/H**).

Now refer this data to Table VI on page 90, and write down the resulting Element. This is the 'Element of Matriculation' or *Kuan Tai* (**S**). The *Kuan Tai* may appear on the juncture between two Elements. If this is the case, note both Elements.

The next step is to draw up a chart, similar to the diagram shown. The Square Base, or Earth Plate, represents the events which take place on Earth. The circular central Heaven Plate represents the orb of the Heavens and the passage of the stellar bodies which regulate our destinies.

Write the numerals I-XII and the names of the corresponding twelve Life-Cycle Palaces round the dial of the Earth Plate, with I (*Kuan Tai*) at the top.

From **S**, we know the 'Element of Matriculation' (*Kuan Tai*): and this should be written on the Heaven Plate at (**a**) next to I. If the *Kuan Tai* lies on the juncture between two Elements, put the names of the adjoining Elements each side of (**a**). Now write the names of the other four Elements, evenly spaced, clockwise around the Heaven Plate, in the correct 'production' order: Wood-Fire-Earth-Metal-Water.

From **R**, we know the Element of Fate, and thus also the Elements associated with the other four Forces. These should now be written in their appropriate positions on the chart, as in the sample below.

Next to each of the Elements, now insert the associated rating, as already determined. (*See* page 78).

The Life-Cycle Chart is now complete and ready to be interpreted.

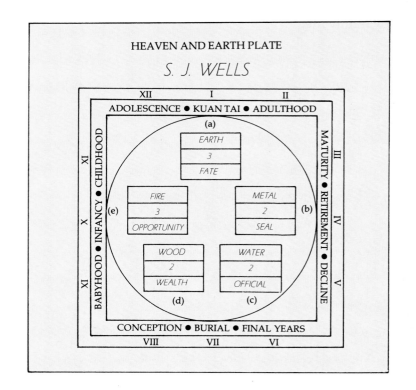

Interpreting the Life-Cycle Chart

There are five possible spheres of activity — or Forces — each reaching a zenith at different times in life. In determining the relevance of these Five Forces, three factors are involved. Firstly, there is the rating of the Element associated with the Force, and this will indicate how strong the Force is. The nature of the Element also gives an indication of the manner in which the Force can be expected to materialise. (If the rating is one, or zero, then it can virtually be ignored.) The Life-Cycle Palaces reveal the period of one's life when this will occur.

The *Fate* determines the relative positions of the other four Forces and is thus the key to the Life-Cycle Chart. It indicates the moment when the direction of life is settled: a stroke of fortune, or a tragedy, the scale and nature of the change being indicated by the rating of the associated Element.

The *Seal* represents family and general happiness. At the end of life, it reveals a contented retirement without regrets. At the beginning, it compensates if other forces are weak; and, whenever it occurs, a strong Seal indicates good health and a happy family life.

The *Wealth* represents riches and material rewards. If it appears around the '*Kuan Tai*' Palace and its associated Element has a high rating, then the querent is destined to become rich. If the Wealth appears at 'Conception', this suggests a prosperous start rather than a life in which money will be earned. Alternatively, an individual whose wealth is indicated at 'Burial' could be destined to make money without being able to enjoy the benefits.

Opportunity offers that unexpected chance which proverbially only knocks once. It differs from the Fate in that it is in no sense inevitable, but is entirely dependent on what use is made of it. For this reason, it is obviously better for Opportunity to be present during early adulthood. If it appears in infancy, then this indicates the continuation of a strong family tradition; if at the end of life, the chance may be passed on to descendants.

The *Official* is a rather more abstruse concept, a legacy from the days when China was ruled by the Mandarins and promotion to office depended on the 'Official' examinations. Today, however, it can be taken to mean all things to do with public office, closely linked with success in examinations, or other 'establishment' spheres, such as politics. Coming at the zenith of the Life-Cycle,

at about the age of twenty-one, it indicates the promise of a particularly successful career. In infancy, it reveals a natural talent; or at the close of life, the promise of public recognition, or even honours.

The Effect of the Five Elements

Each of the Five Forces in the Life-Cycle Chart is associated with one of the Five Elements. By considering the symbolic qualities of the Elements, it is possible to see the form which the different Forces are likely to take. Remember, however, that if the rating of any of the Elements is low in your birth-chart, then its associated Force can be virtually ignored.

The *Wood* Element has a creative, innovative nature, so if it has a high rating, we would expect the associated Force to have an inspirational effect. Wood also indicates good health, a happy family, and numerous descendants. If the overall horoscope element is Water, this is even more fortunate; while if Fire has a high rating, the creative nature of Wood is more likely to be manifested in the arts, rather than family.

The *Fire* Element is one of excitation, energy and stimulus, but it can also be a sign of danger. The experienced astrologer will be able to tell from the predominant Elements in the horoscope whether Fire is in a generative or destructive position. For example, if the Element with the highest rating in the personal horoscope chart is Earth, then Fire will indicate an extremely fortunate period, since Fire produces Earth. If, however, the predominant Element in the chart is Metal, then the Force in which Fire is situated could be a dangerous constituent of the horoscope, since Fire melts Metal, possibly indicating loss of money, or ill-health.

The *Earth* Element refers to land, buildings, construction and real estate. It counsels stability rather than change. It is, however, very fortunate if either Fire or Metal is predominant in the personal horoscope, for then it reveals legacies, or the acquisition of land, depending on the time of life and the associated Force. But if Wood is seen to have an associated high rating, then this may indicate the loss of land.

The *Metal* Element is the sign of harvest, business — and conflicts. At its most basic, this means money, particularly if there is plenty of Earth in the chart to generate the Metal. But Metal also indicates sharpness of a knife; and if Fire has a high rating, this may point to an accident or surgery.

The *Water* Element represents travel, communication, intelligence, and change, indicating correspondence, literature, news and the media generally. Great benefits from abroad can be expected if Metal has an equally high rating in the chart, while travel abroad connected with one's career is revealed by an associated high quotient of Wood. If Earth has a high rating, however, beware of scandal and lawsuits.

How the Elements influence the Five Forces

The following will help the reader to understand how the positive, beneficial influences of the Five Forces are revealed through the Five Elements. Always bear in mind that while a particular Force may not have any significant effect because it is placed before birth, or at the end of life, its associated Element may be prominent enough to have an effect on the rest of the Life-Cycle Chart.

The Fate
A turning point in one's life. In Wood, it refers to creative pursuits; in Fire, a change of direction in career; in Earth, the acquisition of land; in Metal, sudden fortune; in Water, travel.

The Seal
Happiness and contentment. In Wood, it points to pleasures in family life; in Fire, career successes; in Earth, calmness of soul; in Metal, fine possessions; in Water, that one's name will be engraved in a book.

The Official
Social standing. In Wood, it points to honours for artistic achievement; in Fire, for services to the community; in Earth, the award of a title, governorship or diplomatic post; in Metal,
financial support of worthy causes; in Water, scholastic or literary merit.

The Wealth
Material rewards. In Wood, this will be through the arts; in Fire, through management; in Earth, through property; in Metal, through commerce; in Water, through communications. Earth predominant, with Metal in the Wealth, is the combination most likely to indicate riches.

The Opportunity
The timely moment. In Wood, ideas must be put into practice; in Fire, this is the moment to begin a new career; in Earth, a chance to settle in a new location; in Metal, investment at this time will bring riches (the ancient Chinese interpretation was that the moment was right to conquer new territory); in Water, a chance to travel or to further one's education will have a lasting benefit.

For future reference, and also to make the horoscope understandable for friends and others who have not yet studied *Ming Shu — The Art and Practice of Chinese Astrology*, you should write out your interpretation of the Life-Cycle on the horoscope chart. The most convenient way to do this is to summarize the main events in life from childhood to old age, noting the importance and significance of the various Forces which come to bear at different times in life.

Once you have prepared a few horoscopes for friends and other people of your acquaintance, you will soon develop an instinct for interpreting the meanings of the charts. Indeed, you may soon find yourself estimating Element qualities even before you cast a horoscope as such.

Perhaps nothing would be more appropriate to end this book than the opening words of the *Analects* of Confucius:
Learning, perseverance and practice — what could be more satisfying?

TABLE I
Code number for the month

Month	Jan	Feb	Mar	April	May	June	July	Aug	Sept	Oct	Nov	Dec
Code	0	31	59	30	0	31	1	32	3	35	4	34

TABLE II
Code number for the year

Year	1901	1902	1903	1904	1905	1906	1907	1908	1909	1910	1911	1912
Code	15	20	25	30	36	41	46	51	57	2	7	12
Year	1913	1914	1915	1916	1917	1918	1919	1920	1921	1922	1923	1924
Code	18	23	28	33	39	44	49	54	0	5	10	15
Year	1925	1926	1927	1928	1929	1930	1931	1932	1933	1934	1935	1936
Code	21	26	31	36	42	47	52	57	3	8	13	18
Year	1937	1938	1939	1940	1941	1942	1943	1944	1945	1946	1947	1948
Code	24	29	34	39	45	50	55	0	6	11	16	21
Year	1949	1950	1951	1952	1953	1954	1955	1956	1957	1958	1959	1960
Code	27	32	37	42	48	53	58	3	9	14	19	24
Year	1961	1962	1963	1964	1965	1966	1967	1968	1969	1970	1971	1972
Code	30	35	40	45	51	56	1	6	12	17	22	27
Year	1973	1974	1975	1976	1977	1978	1979	1980	1981	1982	1983	1984
Code	33	38	43	48	54	59	4	9	15	20	25	30
Year	1985	1986	1987	1988	1989	1990	1991	1992	1993	1994	1995	1996
Code	36	41	46	51	57	2	7	12	18	23	28	33
Year	1997	1998	1999	2000								
Code	39	44	49	54								

TABLE III
Cyclical number for the time of birth

Stem of the day	11 pm — 1 am	1 am — 3 am	3 am — 5 am	5 am — 7 am	7 am — 9 am	9 am — 11 am	11 am — 1 pm	1 pm — 3 pm	3 pm — 5 pm	5 pm — 7 pm	7 pm — 9 pm	9 pm — 11pm
1	1	2	3	4	5	6	7	8	9	10	11	12
2	13	14	15	16	17	18	19	20	21	22	23	24
3	25	26	27	28	29	30	31	32	33	34	35	36
4	37	38	39	40	41	42	43	44	45	46	47	48
5	49	50	51	52	53	54	55	56	57	58	59	60
6	1	2	3	4	5	6	7	8	9	10	11	12
7	13	14	15	16	17	18	19	20	21	22	23	24
8	25	26	27	28	29	30	31	32	33	34	35	36
9	37	38	39	40	41	42	43	44	45	46	47	48
0	49	50	51	52	53	54	55	56	57	58	59	60

TABLE IV
Chinese Calendar
The Lunar Numbers for the Chinese Months

1st month	Year	2nd	3rd	4th	5th	6th	7th	8th	9th	10th	11th	12th	Year Type	Year Cyclical Number
Feb 19	**1901**	Mar 20	Apr 19	May 18	Jun 16	Jly 16	Aug 14	Sep 13	Oct 12	Nov 11	Dec 11	Jan 10	**Metal-Ox**	38
27		28	29	30	31	32	33	34	35	36	37	38		
Feb 8	**1902**	Mar 10	Apr 8	May 8	Jun 6	Jly 5	Aug 4	Sep 2	Oct 2	Oct 31	Nov 30	Dec 30	**Water-Tiger**	39
39		40	41	42	43	44	45	46	47	48	49	50		
Jan 29	**1903**	Feb 27	Mar 29	Apr 27	May 27	Jly 24	Aug 23	Sep 21	Oct 20	Nov 19	Dec 19	Jan 17	**Water-Hare**	40
51		52	53	54	55*	56	57	58	59	60	1	2		
Feb 16	**1904**	Mar 17	Apr 16	May 15	Jun 14	Jly 13	Aug 11	Sep 10	Oct 9	Nov 7	Dec 7	Jan 6	**Wood-Dragon**	41
3		4	5	6	7	8	9	10	11	12	13	14		
Feb 4	**1905**	Mar 6	Apr 5	May 4	Jun 3	Jly 3	Aug 1	Aug 30	Sep 29	Oct 28	Nov 27	Dec 26	**Wood-Snake**	42
15		16	17	18	19	20	21	22	23	24	25	26		
Jan 25	**1906**	Feb 23	Mar 25	Apr 24	Jun 22	Jly 21	Aug 20	Sep 18	Oct 18	Nov 16	Dec 16	Jan 14	**Fire-Horse**	43
27		28	29	30	31	32	33	34	35	36	37	38		
Feb 13	**1907**	Mar 14	Apr 13	May 12	Jun 11	Jly 10	Aug 9	Sep 8	Oct 7	Nov 6	Dec 5	Jan 4	**Fire-Sheep**	44
39		40	41	42	43	44	45	46	47	48	49	50		
Feb 2	**1908**	Mar 3	Apr 1	Apr 30	May 30	Jun 29	Jly 28	Aug 27	Sep 25	Oct 25	Nov 24	Dec 23	**Earth-Monkey**	45
51		52	53	54	55	56	57	58	59	60	1	2		
Jan 22	**1909**	Feb 20	Apr 20	May 19	Jun 18	Jly 17	Aug 16	Sep 14	Oct 14	Nov 13	Dec 13	Jan 11	**Earth-Rooster**	46
3		4*	5	6	7	8	9	10	11	12	13	14		
Feb 10	**1910**	Mar 11	Apr 10	May 9	Jun 7	Jly 7	Aug 5	Sep 4	Oct 3	Nov 2	Dec 2	Jan 1	**Metal-Dog**	47
15		16	17	18	19	20	21	22	23	24	25	26		
Jan 30	**1911**	Mar 1	Mar 30	Apr 29	May 28	Jun 26	Aug 24	Sep 22	Oct 22	Nov 21	Dec 20	Jan 19	**Metal-Pig**	48
27		28	29	30	31	32*	33	34	35	36	37	38		
Feb 18	**1912**	Mar 19	Apr 17	May 17	Jun 15	Jly 14	Aug 13	Sep 11	Oct 10	Nov 9	Dec 9	Jan 7	**Water-Rat**	49
39		40	41	42	43	44	45	46	47	48	49	50		
Feb 6	**1913**	Mar 8	Apr 7	May 6	Jun 5	Jly 4	Aug 2	Sep 1	Sep 30	Oct 29	Nov 28	Dec 27	**Water-Ox**	50
51		52	53	54	55	56	57	58	59	60	1	2		
Jan 26	**1914**	Feb 25	Mar 27	Apr 25	May 25	Jly 23	Aug 21	Sep 20	Oct 19	Nov 18	Dec 17	Jan 15	**Wood-Tiger**	51
3		4	5	6	7*	8	9	10	11	12	13	14		
Feb 14	**1915**	Mar 16	Apr 14	May 14	Jun 13	Jly 12	Aug 11	Sep 9	Oct 9	Nov 7	Dec 7	Jan 5	**Wood-Hare**	52
15		16	17	18	19	20	21	22	23	24	25	26		
Feb 3	**1916**	Mar 4	Apr 3	May 2	Jun 1	Jun 30	Jly 30	Aug 30	Sep 27	Oct 27	Nov 25	Dec 25	**Fire-Dragon**	53
27		28	29	30	31	32	33	34	35	36	37	38		
Jan 23	**1917**	Feb 22	Apr 21	May 21	Jun 19	Jly 19	Aug 18	Sep 16	Oct 16	Nov 15	Dec 14	Jan 13	**Fire-Snake**	54
39		40*	41	42	43	44	45	46	47	48	49	50		
Feb 11	**1918**	Mar 13	Apr 11	May 10	Jun 9	Jly 8	Aug 7	Sep 5	Oct 5	Nov 4	Dec 3	Jan 2	**Earth-Horse**	55
51		52	53	54	55	56	57	58	59	60	1	2		
Feb 1	**1919**	Mar 2	Apr 1	Apr 30	May 29	Jun 28	Jly 27	Sep 24	Oct 24	Nov 22	Dec 22	Jan 21	**Earth-Sheep**	56
3		4	5	6	7	8	9*	10	11	12	13	14		
Feb 20	**1920**	Mar 20	Apr 19	May 18	Jun 16	Jly 16	Aug 14	Sep 12	Oct 12	Nov 11	Dec 10	Jan 9	**Metal-Monkey**	57
15		16	17	18	19	20	21	22	23	24	25	26		

Year	1st month	2nd	3rd	4th	5th	6th	7th	8th	9th	10th	11th	12th	Year Type	Year Cyclical Number
1921	Feb 8 (27)	Mar 10 (28)	Apr 8 (29)	May 8 (30)	Jun 6 (31)	Jly 5 (32)	Aug 4 (33)	Sep 2 (34)	Oct 1 (35)	Oct 31 (36)	Nov 29 (37)	Dec 29 (38)	**Metal-Rooster**	58
1922	Jan 28 (39)	Feb 27 (40)	Mar 28 (41)	Apr 27 (42)	May 27 (43*)	Jly 24 (44)	Aug 23 (45)	Sep 21 (46)	Oct 20 (47)	Nov 19 (48)	Dec 18 (49)	Jan 17 (50)	**Water-Dog**	59
1923	Feb 16 (51)	Mar 17 (52)	Apr 16 (53)	May 16 (54)	Jun 14 (55)	Jly 14 (56)	Aug 12 (57)	Sep 11 (58)	Oct 10 (59)	Nov 8 (60)	Dec 8 (1)	Jan 6 (2)	**Water-Pig**	60
1924	Feb 5 (3)	Mar 6 (4)	Apr 4 (5)	May 4 (6)	Jun 2 (7)	Jly 2 (8)	Aug 1 (9)	Aug 30 (10)	Sep 29 (11)	Oct 28 (12)	Nov 27 (13)	Dec 26 (14)	**Wood-Rat**	1
1925	Jan 25 (15)	Feb 23 (16)	Mar 24 (17)	Apr 23 (18*)	Jun 21 (19)	Jly 21 (20)	Aug 19 (21)	Sep 18 (22)	Oct 18 (23)	Nov 16 (24)	Dec 16 (25)	Jan 14 (26)	**Wood-Ox**	2
1926	Feb 13 (27)	Mar 14 (28)	Apr 12 (29)	May 12 (30)	Jun 10 (31)	Jly 10 (32)	Aug 8 (33)	Sep 7 (34)	Oct 7 (35)	Nov 5 (36)	Dec 5 (37)	Jan 4 (38)	**Fire-Tiger**	3
1927	Feb 2 (39)	Mar 4 (40)	Apr 2 (41)	May 1 (42)	May 31 (43)	Jun 29 (44)	Jly 29 (45)	Aug 27 (46)	Sep 26 (47)	Oct 26 (48)	Nov 24 (49)	Dec 24 (50)	**Fire-Rabbit**	4
1928	Jan 23 (51)	Feb 21 (52*)	Apr 20 (53)	May 19 (54)	Jun 18 (55)	Jly 17 (56)	Aug 15 (57)	Sep 14 (58)	Oct 13 (59)	Nov 12 (60)	Dec 12 (1)	Jan 11 (2)	**Earth-Dragon**	5
1929	Feb 10 (3)	Mar 11 (4)	Apr 10 (5)	May 9 (6)	Jun 7 (7)	Jly 7 (8)	Aug 5 (9)	Sep 3 (10)	Oct 3 (11)	Nov 1 (12)	Dec 1 (13)	Dec 31 (14)	**Earth-Snake**	6
1930	Jan 30 (15)	Feb 28 (16)	Mar 30 (17)	Apr 29 (18)	May 28 (19)	Jun 26 (20*)	Aug 24 (21)	Sep 22 (22)	Oct 22 (23)	Nov 20 (24)	Dec 20 (25)	Jan 19 (26)	**Metal-Horse**	7
1931	Feb 17 (27)	Mar 19 (28)	Apr 18 (29)	May 17 (30)	Jun 16 (31)	Jly 15 (32)	Aug 14 (33)	Sep 12 (34)	Oct 11 (35)	Nov 10 (36)	Dec 9 (37)	Jan 8 (38)	**Metal-Sheep**	8
1932	Feb 6 (39)	Mar 7 (40)	Apr 6 (41)	May 6 (42)	Jun 4 (43)	Jly 4 (44)	Aug 2 (45)	Sep 1 (46)	Sep 30 (47)	Oct 29 (48)	Nov 28 (49)	Dec 27 (50)	**Water-Monkey**	9
1933	Jan 26 (51)	Feb 24 (52)	Mar 26 (53)	Apr 25 (54)	May 24 (55*)	Jly 23 (56)	Aug 21 (57)	Sep 20 (58)	Oct 19 (59)	Nov 18 (60)	Dec 17 (1)	Jan 15 (2)	**Water-Rooster**	10
1934	Feb 14 (3)	Mar 15 (4)	Apr 14 (5)	May 13 (6)	Jun 12 (7)	Jly 12 (8)	Aug 10 (9)	Sep 9 (10)	Oct 8 (11)	Nov 7 (12)	Dec 7 (13)	Jan 5 (14)	**Wood-Dog**	11
1935	Feb 4 (15)	Mar 5 (16)	Apr 3 (17)	May 3 (18)	Jun 1 (19)	Jly 1 (20)	Jly 30 (21)	Aug 29 (22)	Sep 28 (23)	Oct 27 (24)	Nov 26 (25)	Dec 26 (26)	**Wood-Pig**	12
1936	Jan 24 (27)	Feb 23 (28)	Mar 23 (29*)	May 21 (30)	Jun 19 (31)	Jly 18 (32)	Aug 17 (33)	Sep 16 (34)	Oct 15 (35)	Nov 14 (36)	Dec 14 (37)	Jan 13 (38)	**Fire-Rat**	13
1937	Feb 11 (39)	Mar 13 (40)	Apr 11 (41)	May 10 (42)	Jun 9 (43)	Jly 8 (44)	Aug 6 (45)	Sep 5 (46)	Oct 4 (47)	Nov 3 (48)	Dec 3 (49)	Jan 2 (50)	**Fire-Ox**	14
1938	Jan 31 (51)	Mar 2 (52)	Apr 1 (53)	Apr 30 (54)	May 29 (55)	Jun 28 (56)	Jly 27 (57*)	Sep 24 (58)	Oct 23 (59)	Nov 22 (60)	Dec 22 (1)	Jan 20 (2)	**Earth-Tiger**	15
1939	Feb 19 (3)	Mar 21 (4)	Apr 20 (5)	May 19 (6)	Jun 17 (7)	Jly 17 (8)	Aug 15 (9)	Sep 13 (10)	Oct 13 (11)	Nov 11 (12)	Dec 11 (13)	Jan 9 (14)	**Earth-Hare**	16
1940	Feb 8 (15)	Mar 9 (16)	Apr 8 (17)	May 7 (18)	Jun 6 (19)	Jly 5 (20)	Aug 4 (21)	Sep 2 (22)	Oct 1 (23)	Oct 31 (24)	Nov 29 (25)	Dec 29 (26)	**Metal-Dragon**	17

(* denotes an intercalary month; i.e. the month is 'repeated' in order to bring the calendar into line with the seasons of the year, so accounting for what appears to be an inordinately long month).

1st month		2nd	3rd	4th	5th	6th	7th	8th	9th	10th	11th	12th	Year Type	Year Cyclical Number
Jan 27 / 27	**1941**	Feb 26 / 28	Mar 28 / 29	Apr 26 / 30	May 26 / 31	Jun 25 / 32*	Aug 23 / 33	Sep 21 / 34	Oct 20 / 35	Nov 19 / 36	Dec 18 / 37	Jan 17 / 38	**Metal-Snake**	18
Feb 15 / 39	**1942**	Mar 17 / 40	Apr 15 / 41	May 15 / 42	Jun 14 / 43	Jly 13 / 44	Aug 12 / 45	Sep 10 / 46	Oct 10 / 47	Nov 8 / 48	Dec 8 / 49	Jan 6 / 50	**Water-Horse**	19
Feb 5 / 51	**1943**	Mar 6 / 52	Apr 5 / 53	May 4 / 54	Jun 3 / 55	Jly 2 / 56	Aug 1 / 57	Aug 31 / 58	Sep 29 / 59	Oct 29 / 60	Nov 27 / 1	Dec 27 / 2	**Water-Sheep**	20
Jan 25 / 3	**1944**	Feb 24 / 4	Mar 24 / 5	Apr 23 / 6	Jun 21 / 7*	Jly 20 / 8	Aug 19 / 9	Sep 17 / 10	Oct 17 / 11	Nov 16 / 12	Dec 15 / 13	Jan 14 / 14	**Wood-Monkey**	21
Feb 13 / 15	**1945**	Mar 14 / 16	Apr 12 / 17	May 12 / 18	Jun 10 / 19	Jly 9 / 20	Aug 8 / 21	Sep 6 / 22	Oct 6 / 23	Nov 5 / 24	Dec 5 / 25	Jan 3 / 26	**Wood-Rooster**	22
Feb 2 / 27	**1946**	Mar 4 / 28	Apr 2 / 29	May 1 / 30	May 31 / 31	Jun 29 / 32	Jly 28 / 33	Aug 27 / 34	Sep 25 / 35	Oct 25 / 36	Nov 24 / 37	Dec 23 / 38	**Fire-Dog**	23
Jan 22 / 39	**1947**	Feb 21 / 40*	Apr 21 / 41	May 20 / 42	Jun 19 / 43	Jly 18 / 44	Aug 16 / 45	Sep 15 / 46	Oct 14 / 47	Nov 13 / 48	Dec 12 / 49	Jan 11 / 50	**Fire-Pig**	24
Feb 10 / 51	**1948**	Mar 11 / 52	Apr 9 / 53	May 9 / 54	Jun 7 / 55	Jly 7 / 56	Aug 5 / 57	Sep 3 / 58	Oct 3 / 59	Nov 1 / 60	Dec 1 / 1	Dec 30 / 2	**Earth-Rat**	25
Jan 29 / 3	**1949**	Feb 28 / 4	Mar 29 / 5	Apr 28 / 6	May 28 / 7	Jun 26 / 8	Jly 26 / 9*	Sep 22 / 10	Oct 22 / 11	Nov 20 / 12	Dec 20 / 13	Jan 18 / 14	**Earth-Ox**	26
Feb 17 / 15	**1950**	Mar 18 / 16	Apr 17 / 17	May 17 / 18	Jun 15 / 19	Jly 15 / 20	Aug 14 / 21	Sep 12 / 22	Oct 11 / 23	Nov 10 / 24	Dec 9 / 25	Jan 8 / 26	**Metal-Tiger**	27
Feb 6 / 27	**1951**	Mar 8 / 28	Apr 6 / 29	May 6 / 30	Jun 5 / 31	Jly 4 / 32	Aug 3 / 33	Sep 1 / 34	Oct 1 / 35	Oct 30 / 36	Nov 29 / 37	Dec 28 / 38	**Metal-Hare**	28
Jan 27 / 39	**1952**	Feb 25 / 40	Mar 26 / 41	Apr 24 / 42	May 24 / 43*	Jly 22 / 44	Aug 20 / 45	Sep 19 / 46	Oct 19 / 47	Nov 17 / 48	Dec 17 / 49	Jan 15 / 50	**Water-Dragon**	29
Feb 14 / 51	**1953**	Mar 15 / 52	Apr 14 / 53	May 13 / 54	Jun 11 / 55	Jly 11 / 56	Aug 9 / 57	Sep 8 / 58	Oct 8 / 59	Nov 7 / 60	Dec 6 / 1	Jan 5 / 2	**Water-Snake**	30
Feb 3 / 3	**1954**	Mar 5 / 4	Apr 4 / 5	May 3 / 6	Jun 1 / 7	Jun 30 / 8	Jly 30 / 9	Aug 28 / 10	Sep 27 / 11	Oct 27 / 12	Nov 25 / 13	Dec 25 / 14	**Wood-Horse**	31
Jan 24 / 15	**1955**	Feb 22 / 16	Mar 24 / 17*	May 22 / 18	Jun 20 / 19	Jly 19 / 20	Aug 18 / 21	Sep 16 / 22	Oct 16 / 23	Nov 14 / 24	Dec 14 / 25	Jan 13 / 26	**Wood-Sheep**	32
Feb 12 / 27	**1956**	Mar 12 / 28	Apr 11 / 29	May 10 / 30	Jun 9 / 31	Jly 8 / 32	Aug 6 / 33	Sep 5 / 34	Oct 4 / 35	Nov 3 / 36	Dec 2 / 37	Jan 1 / 38	**Fire-Monkey**	33
Jan 31 / 39	**1957**	Mar 2 / 40	Mar 31 / 41	Apr 30 / 42	May 29 / 43	Jun 28 / 44	Jly 27 / 45	Aug 25 / 46*	Oct 23 / 47	Nov 22 / 48	Dec 21 / 49	Jan 20 / 50	**Fire-Rooster**	34
Feb 18 / 51	**1958**	Mar 20 / 52	Apr 19 / 53	May 19 / 54	Jun 17 / 55	Jly 17 / 56	Aug 15 / 57	Sep 13 / 58	Oct 13 / 59	Nov 11 / 60	Dec 11 / 1	Jan 9 / 2	**Earth-Dog**	35
Feb 8 / 3	**1959**	Mar 9 / 4	Apr 8 / 5	May 8 / 6	Jun 6 / 7	Jly 6 / 8	Aug 4 / 9	Sep 3 / 10	Oct 2 / 11	Nov 1 / 12	Dec 1 / 13	Dec 30 / 14	**Earth-Pig**	36
Jan 28 / 15	**1960**	Feb 27 / 16	Mar 27 / 17	Apr 26 / 18	May 25 / 19	Jun 24 / 20*	Aug 22 / 21	Sep 21 / 22	Oct 20 / 23	Nov 19 / 24	Dec 18 / 25	Jan 17 / 26	**Metal-Rat**	37
Feb 15 / 27	**1961**	Mar 17 / 28	Apr 15 / 29	May 15 / 30	Jun 13 / 31	Jly 13 / 32	Aug 11 / 33	Sep 10 / 34	Oct 10 / 35	Nov 8 / 36	Dec 9 / 37	Jan 6 / 38	**Metal-Ox**	38

1st month		2nd	3rd	4th	5th	6th	7th	8th	9th	10th	11th	12th	Year Type	Year Cyclical Number
Feb 5 39	1962	Mar 6 40	Apr 5 41	May 4 42	Jun 2 43	Jly 2 44	Jly 31 45	Aug 30 46	Sep 29 47	Oct 28 48	Nov 27 49	Dec 27 50	**Water-Tiger**	39
Jan 25 51	1963	Feb 24 52	Mar 25 53	Apr 24 54*	Jun 21 55	Jly 21 56	Aug 19 57	Sep 18 58	Oct 17 59	Nov 16 60	Dec 16 1	Jan 15 2	**Water-Hare**	40
Feb 13 3	1964	Mar 14 4	Apr 12 5	May 12 6	Jun 10 7	Jly 9 8	Aug 8 9	Sep 6 10	Oct 6 11	Nov 4 12	Dec 4 13	Jan 3 14	**Wood-Dragon**	41
Feb 2 15	1965	Mar 3 16	Apr 2 17	May 1 18	May 31 19	Jun 29 20	Jly 28 21	Aug 27 22	Sep 25 23	Oct 24 24	Nov 23 25	Dec 23 26	**Wood-Snake**	42
Jan 21 27	1966	Feb 20 28	Mar 22 29*	May 20 30	Jun 19 31	Jly 18 32	Aug 16 33	Sep 15 34	Oct 14 35	Nov 12 36	Dec 12 37	Jan 11 38	**Fire-Horse**	43
Feb 9 39	1967	Mar 11 40	Apr 10 41	May 9 42	Jun 8 43	Jly 8 44	Aug 6 45	Sep 4 46	Oct 4 47	Nov 2 48	Dec 2 49	Dec 31 50	**Fire-Sheep**	44
Jan 30 51	1968	Feb 28 52	Mar 29 53	Apr 27 54	May 27 55	Jun 26 56	Jly 25 57*	Sep 22 58	Oct 22 59	Nov 20 60	Dec 20 1	Jan 18 2	**Earth-Monkey**	45
Feb 17 3	1969	Mar 18 4	Apr 17 5	May 16 6	Jun 15 7	Jly 14 8	Aug 13 9	Sep 12 10	Oct 11 11	Nov 10 12	Dec 9 13	Jan 8 14	**Earth-Rooster**	46
Feb 6 15	1970	Mar 8 16	Apr 6 17	May 5 18	Jun 4 19	Jly 3 20	Aug 2 21	Sep 1 22	Sep 30 23	Oct 30 24	Nov 29 25	Dec 28 26	**Metal-Dog**	47
Jan 27 27	1971	Feb 25 28	Mar 27 29	Apr 25 30	May 24 31*	Jly 22 32	Aug 21 33	Sep 19 34	Oct 19 35	Nov 18 36	Dec 18 37	Jan 16 38	**Metal-Pig**	48
Feb 15 39	1972	Mar 15 40	Apr 14 41	May 13 42	Jun 11 43	Jly 11 44	Aug 9 45	Sep 8 46	Oct 7 47	Nov 6 48	Dec 6 49	Jan 4 50	**Water-Rat**	49
Feb 3 51	1973	Mar 5 52	Apr 3 53	May 3 54	Jun 1 55	Jun 30 56	Jly 30 57	Aug 28 58	Sep 26 59	Oct 26 60	Nov 25 1	Dec 24 2	**Water-Ox**	50
Jan 23 3	1974	Feb 22 4	Mar 24 5	Apr 22 6*	Jun 20 7	Jly 19 8	Aug 18 9	Sep 16 10	Oct 15 11	Nov 14 12	Dec 14 13	Jan 12 14	**Wood-Tiger**	51
Feb 11 15	1975	Mar 13 16	Apr 12 17	May 11 18	Jun 10 19	Jly 9 20	Aug 7 21	Sep 6 22	Oct 5 23	Nov 3 24	Dec 3 25	Jan 1 26	**Wood-Hare**	52
Jan 31 27	1976	Mar 1 28	Mar 31 29	Apr 29 30	May 29 31	Jun 27 32	Jly 27 33	Aug 25 34*	Oct 23 35	Nov 21 36	Dec 21 37	Jan 19 38	**Fire-Dragon**	53
Feb 18 39	1977	Mar 20 40	Apr 18 41	May 18 42	Jun 17 43	Jly 16 44	Aug 15 45	Sep 13 46	Oct 13 47	Nov 11 48	Dec 11 49	Jan 9 50	**Fire-Snake**	54
Feb 7 51	1978	Mar 9 52	Apr 7 53	May 7 54	Jun 6 55	Jly 5 56	Aug 4 57	Sep 2 58	Oct 2 59	Nov 1 60	Nov 30 1	Dec 30 2	**Earth-Horse**	55
Jan 28 3	1979	Feb 27 4	Mar 28 5	Apr 26 6	May 26 7	Jun 24 8*	Aug 23 9	Sep 21 10	Oct 21 11	Nov 20 12	Dec 19 13	Jan 18 14	**Earth-Sheep**	56
Feb 16 15	1980	Mar 17 16	Apr 15 17	May 14 18	Jun 13 19	Jly 12 20	Aug 11 21	Sep 9 22	Oct 9 23	Nov 8 24	Dec 7 25	Jan 6 26	**Metal-Monkey**	57
Feb 5 27	1981	Mar 6 28	Apr 5 29	May 4 30	Jun 2 31	Jly 2 32	Jly 31 33	Aug 29 34	Sep 28 35	Oct 28 36	Nov 26 37	Dec 26 38	**Metal-Rooster**	58

(* denotes an intercalary month; i.e. the month is 'repeated' in order to bring the calendar into line with the seasons of the year, so accounting for what appears to be an inordinately long month).

Year	1st month	2nd	3rd	4th	5th	6th	7th	8th	9th	10th	11th	12th	Year Type	Year Cyclical Number
1982	Jan 25 (39)	Feb 24 (40)	Mar 25 (41)	Apr 24 (42*)	Jun 21 (43)	Jly 21 (44)	Aug 19 (45)	Sep 17 (46)	Oct 17 (47)	Nov 15 (48)	Dec 15 (49)	Jan 14 (50)	**Water-Dog**	59
1983	Feb 13 (51)	Mar 15 (52)	Apr 13 (53)	May 13 (54)	Jun 11 (55)	Jly 10 (56)	Aug 9 (57)	Sep 7 (58)	Oct 6 (59)	Nov 5 (60)	Dec 4 (1)	Jan 3 (2)	**Water-Pig**	60
1984	Feb 2 (3)	Mar 3 (4)	Apr 1 (5)	May 1 (6)	May 31 (7)	Jun 29 (8)	Jly 28 (9)	Aug 27 (10)	Sep 25 (11)	Oct 24 (12*)	Dec 22 (13)	Jan 21 (14)	**Wood-Rat**	1
1985	Feb 20 (15)	Mar 21 (16)	Apr 20 (17)	May 20 (18)	Jun 18 (19)	Jly 18 (20)	Aug 16 (21)	Sep 15 (22)	Oct 14 (23)	Nov 12 (24)	Dec 12 (25)	Jan 10 (26)	**Wood-Ox**	2
1986	Feb 9 (27)	Mar 10 (28)	April 9 (29)	May 9 (30)	Jun 7 (31)	Jly 7 (32)	Aug 6 (33)	Sep 4 (34)	Oct 4 (35)	Nov 2 (36)	Dec 2 (37)	Dec 31 (38)	**Fire-Tiger**	3
1987	Jan 29 (39)	Feb 28 (40)	Mar 29 (41)	Apr 28 (42)	May 27 (43)	Jun 26 (44*)	Aug 24 (45)	Sep 23 (46)	Oct 23 (47)	Nov 21 (48)	Dec 21 (49)	Jan 19 (50)	**Fire-Hare**	4
1988	Feb 17 (51)	Mar 18 (52)	Apr 16 (53)	May 16 (54)	Jun 14 (55)	Jly 14 (56)	Aug 12 (57)	Sep 11 (58)	Oct 11 (59)	Nov 9 (60)	Dec 9 (1)	Jan 8 (2)	**Earth-Dragon**	5
1989	Feb 6 (3)	Mar 8 (4)	Apr 6 (5)	May 5 (6)	Jun 4 (7)	Jly 3 (8)	Aug 1 (9)	Aug 31 (10)	Sep 30 (11)	Oct 29 (12)	Nov 28 (13)	Dec 28 (14)	**Earth-Snake**	6
1990	Jan 27 (15)	Feb 25 (16)	Mar 27 (17)	Apr 25 (18)	May 24 (19*)	Jly 22 (20)	Aug 20 (21)	Sep 19 (22)	Oct 18 (23)	Nov 17 (24)	Dec 17 (25)	Jan 16 (26)	**Metal-Horse**	7
1991	Feb 15 (27)	Mar 16 (28)	Apr 15 (29)	May 14 (30)	Jun 12 (31)	Jly 12 (32)	Aug 10 (33)	Sep 8 (34)	Oct 8 (35)	Nov 6 (36)	Dec 6 (37)	Jan 5 (38)	**Metal-Sheep**	8
1992	Feb 4 (39)	Mar 4 (40)	Apr 3 (41)	May 3 (42)	Jun 1 (43)	Jun 30 (44)	Jly 30 (45)	Aug 28 (46)	Sep 26 (47)	Oct 26 (48)	Nov 24 (49)	Dec 24 (50)	**Water-Monkey**	9
1993	Jan 23 (51)	Feb 21 (52)	Mar 23 (53*)	May 21 (54)	Jun 20 (55)	Jly 19 (56)	Aug 18 (57)	Sep 16 (58)	Oct 15 (59)	Nov 14 (60)	Dec 13 (1)	Jan 12 (2)	**Water-Rooster**	10
1994	Feb 10 (3)	Mar 12 (4)	Apr 11 (5)	May 11 (6)	Jun 9 (7)	Jly 9 (8)	Aug 7 (9)	Sep 6 (10)	Oct 5 (11)	Nov 3 (12)	Dec 3 (13)	Jan 1 (14)	**Wood-Dog**	11
1995	Jan 31 (15)	Mar 1 (16)	Mar 31 (17)	Apr 30 (18)	May 29 (19)	Jun 28 (20)	Jly 27 (21)	Aug 26 (22*)	Oct 24 (23)	Nov 22 (24)	Dec 22 (25)	Jan 20 (26)	**Wood-Pig**	12
1996	Feb 19 (27)	Mar 19 (28)	Apr 18 (29)	May 17 (30)	Jun 16 (31)	Jly 16 (32)	Aug 14 (33)	Sep 13 (34)	Oct 12 (35)	Nov 11 (36)	Dec 11 (37)	Jan 9 (38)	**Fire-Rat**	13
1997	Feb 7 (39)	Mar 9 (40)	Apr 7 (41)	May 7 (42)	Jun 5 (43)	Jly 5 (44)	Aug 3 (45)	Sep 2 (46)	Oct 2 (47)	Oct 31 (48)	Nov 30 (49)	Dec 30 (50)	**Fire-Ox**	14
1998	Jan 28 (51)	Feb 27 (52)	Mar 28 (53)	Apr 26 (54)	May 26 (55*)	Jly 23 (56)	Aug 22 (57)	Sep 21 (58)	Oct 20 (59)	Nov 19 (60)	Dec 19 (1)	Jan 17 (2)	**Earth-Tiger**	15
1999	Feb 16 (3)	Mar 18 (4)	Apr 16 (5)	May 15 (6)	Jun 14 (7)	Jly 13 (8)	Aug 11 (9)	Sep 10 (10)	Oct 9 (11)	Nov 8 (12)	Dec 8 (13)	Jan 7 (14)	**Earth-Hare**	16
2000	Feb 5 (15)	Mar 6 (16)	Apr 5 (17)	May 4 (18)	Jun 2 (19)	Jly 2 (20)	Jly 31 (21)	Aug 29 (22)	Sep 28 (23)	Oct 27 (24)	Nov 26 (25)	Dec 26 (26)	**Metal-Dragon**	17

(* denotes an intercalary month; i.e. the month is 'repeated' in order to bring the calendar into line with the seasons of the year, so accounting for what appears to be an inordinately long month).

TABLE V

To find the Stem, Branch and Elements for each Pillar of Fate

Cyclical Number	Stem	Branch	Stem Element	Branch Element	Stem-and-Branch Element	Cyclical Number	Stem	Branch	Stem Element	Branch Element	Stem-and-Branch Element
GELH	M	N	O	P	Q	GELH	M	N	O	P	Q
1	1	I	WOOD	WATER	METAL	31	1	VII	WOOD	FIRE	METAL
2	2	II	WOOD	EARTH	METAL	32	2	VIII	WOOD	EARTH	METAL
3	3	III	FIRE	WOOD	FIRE	33	3	IX	FIRE	METAL	FIRE
4	4	IV	FIRE	WOOD	FIRE	34	4	X	FIRE	METAL	FIRE
5	5	V	EARTH	EARTH	WOOD	35	5	XI	EARTH	EARTH	WOOD
6	6	VI	EARTH	FIRE	WOOD	36	6	XII	EARTH	WATER	WOOD
7	7	VII	METAL	FIRE	EARTH	37	7	I	METAL	WATER	EARTH
8	8	VIII	METAL	EARTH	EARTH	38	8	II	METAL	EARTH	EARTH
9	9	IX	WATER	METAL	METAL	39	9	III	WATER	WOOD	METAL
10	10	X	WATER	METAL	METAL	40	10	IV	WATER	WOOD	METAL
11	1	XI	WOOD	EARTH	FIRE	41	1	V	WOOD	EARTH	FIRE
12	2	XII	WOOD	WATER	FIRE	42	2	VI	WOOD	FIRE	FIRE
13	3	I	FIRE	WATER	WATER	43	3	VII	FIRE	FIRE	WATER
14	4	II	FIRE	EARTH	WATER	44	4	VIII	FIRE	EARTH	WATER
15	5	III	EARTH	WOOD	EARTH	45	5	IX	EARTH	METAL	EARTH
16	6	IV	EARTH	WOOD	EARTH	46	6	X	EARTH	METAL	EARTH
17	7	V	METAL	EARTH	METAL	47	7	XI	METAL	EARTH	METAL
18	8	VI	METAL	FIRE	METAL	48	8	XII	METAL	WATER	METAL
19	9	VII	WATER	FIRE	WOOD	49	9	I	WATER	WATER	WOOD
20	10	VIII	WATER	EARTH	WOOD	50	10	II	WATER	EARTH	WOOD
21	1	IX	WOOD	METAL	WATER	51	1	III	WOOD	WOOD	WATER
22	2	X	WOOD	METAL	WATER	52	2	IV	WOOD	WOOD	WATER
23	3	XI	FIRE	EARTH	EARTH	53	3	V	FIRE	EARTH	EARTH
24	4	XII	FIRE	WATER	EARTH	54	4	VI	FIRE	FIRE	EARTH
25	5	I	EARTH	WATER	FIRE	55	5	VII	EARTH	FIRE	FIRE
26	6	II	EARTH	EARTH	FIRE	56	6	VIII	EARTH	EARTH	FIRE
27	7	III	METAL	WOOD	WOOD	57	7	IX	METAL	METAL	WOOD
28	8	IV	METAL	WOOD	WOOD	58	8	X	METAL	METAL	WOOD
29	9	V	WATER	EARTH	WATER	59	9	XI	WATER	EARTH	WATER
30	10	VI	WATER	FIRE	WATER	60	10	XII	WATER	WATER	WATER

TABLE VI
To find the Element of Matriculation (S)

[90]

GLOSSARY

Branches, Twelve Earthly Twelve symbols used to number the twelve Chinese double-hours, the months of the Chinese year and the years of the *Great Year*.

Buddhism One of the three predominant religions of China, introduced there in the first century, during the reign of the Emperor Ming Ti (58-76AD).

Confucius K'ung Fu Tze, China's greatest sage, 551-478BC, whose sayings were collected by his disciples into the *Analects*.

Earth Currents The complementary science to astrology is geomancy, known to the Chinese as *Feng Shui* meaning 'Wind and Water'. Lines of force, *Ch'i*, or 'Earth currents', are believed to be affected, adversely or beneficially, by changes to the earth's natural shape through excavation or building.

Elements, Five The Chinese philosophy of the *Five Elements* — Wood, Fire, Earth, Metal, Water — holds that all action is due to a shift in balance between these five principles. In Chinese astrology, the proportions of each element in a horoscope are the keys to the personality and fortune of the individual.

Equinox This term refers to two days of the year — one in spring (around 21 March) and one in autumn (around 22 September) — when day and night of are of equal duration.

Fortunate (and unfortunate) days Certain days are regarded as being more or less fortunate, depending on whether the *Stem* and *Branch* of the day harmonise with the components of the personal horoscope.

Great Year The time taken by the planet Jupiter to complete its orbit of the skies, equal to twelve ordinary years, traditionally regarded by the Chinese as being 'months' of the *Great Year*. About 1000 years ago, astrologers in northern China named the twelve 'Great Months' after their totem animals from which the Chinese Zodiac is derived. *See also Palaces*.

I Ching ('*The Book of Changes*') A mystic book of divination, one of the Five Sacred Classics, with no equivalent in any Western literature. It is accepted as being one of the oldest Chinese texts in existence.

Kuan Tai *Kuan Tai* (literally 'cap and sash') is the moment when schooling or apprenticeship is complete — generally around the age of twenty-one.

Life-Cycle Chart A characteristic feature of Chinese horoscopes which reveals the major events in life, from birth to old age.

Palaces, The Twelve The twelve stages, or periods of personal existence, of unequal duration but generally of equal significance: Conception, Birth, Infancy, Childhood, Adolescence, *Kuan Tai*, Adulthood, Maturity, Retirement, Decline, Final Years, Burial.

Pillars, The Four The basic components of a Chinese horoscope are the *Four Pillars*. These are the foundation for all further calculations to determine character, compatibility and destiny. The *Four Pillars* themselves are the hour, the day, the month, and the year of birth, expressed in *Stems* and *Branches*.

Querent A useful term employed by astrologers to mean the person whose horoscope is being cast.

Rites, The Book of One of the Five Sacred Classics, assembled in the Han dynasty (207-93BC) from earlier sources. It sets out the pious and mundane duties for each month of the year for everyone from Emperor to convicted criminal.

Seasons, The Five The Chinese allocate the four seasons to the four Elements Wood, Fire, Metal and Water, which leaves one Element, Earth, without a season. The 'Earth Season' is sometimes regarded as being the 'Indian summer' or hot spell which preceeds the onset of autumn.

Solstice The longest day of the year is known as the *Summer Solstice*, and the shortest as the *Winter Solstice*.

Stems, The Ten Heavenly A sequence of ten symbols originally devised for reckoning the days of the Chinese 'ten-day week', the *Ten Heavenly Stems* became a basic device in Chinese astrological calculations.

T'ai Sui Literally, the *Great Year*, but often used by Chinese astrologers to mean an imaginary planet which orbits the Heavens in a reverse direction to the planet Jupiter. Its position marks the year of the Chinese calendar.

Yang, Yin The positive and negative influences which permeate all matter and energy, often interpreted as having 'masculine' and 'feminine' qualities.

CHINESE HOROSCOPE

S. J. WELLS

Time and Date of Birth

3·20 am/23rd October 1952

Chinese Hour and Date of Birth

3rd	*5th*	*9th*	*WATER-DRAGON*
HOUR	**DAY**	**MONTH**	**YEAR-TYPE**

The Four Pillars

3	*1*	*7*	*9*
III	*V*	*XI*	*V*

Elements for Each Pillar

Fire	*Wood*	*Metal*	*Water*
Wood	*Earth*	*Earth*	*Earth*
Fire	*Fire*	*Metal*	*Water*

WOOD	FIRE	EARTH	METAL	WATER
2	*3*	*3*	*2*	*2*

Personality Summary

Animal-Type

DRAGON

Flamboyant and extrovert in character. A lover of the exotic. Innovative fashion sense. Fertile imagination: a dreamer at times. Strong, resolute and determined. However, somewhat extravagant.

鼠牛虎兔龍蛇
馬羊猴鶏犬豬

The Five Elements

Even proportion of the Five Elements indicates a well-balanced, yet versatile personality and fruitful life. Rating of 3 for <u>Earth</u> reveals a practicality and reliability otherwise generally lacking in the Dragon-personality; while the rating of 3 for <u>Fire</u> shows just what a vigorous and spirited Dragon this is!

木火土金水

Fortunate Stems

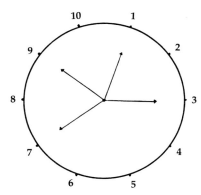

Indications:

Stems 7, 9, 1, 3 form a regular pattern, revealing the querent to be someone destined to succeed in life.

Harmonious Branches

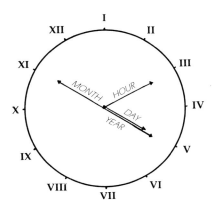

Indications:

The harmonious aspects formed by month and hour, hour and day, and hour and year Branches more than adequately compensate for conflict shown by month Branch being in opposition to day and year Branches.

The Life-Cycle Chart

	Element		Element
Fate	Earth	**Wealth**	Wood
Seal	Metal	**Opportunity**	Fire
Official	Water	**Kuan Tai**	Earth

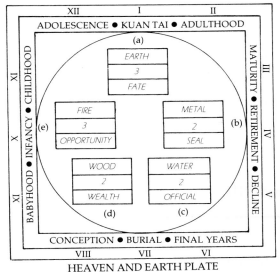

Interpretation of the Life-Cycle Chart

Wealth in Babyhood indicates comfortable start in life. High rating of Fire, associated with Opportunity in Adolescence, shows success at school. Fate in Earth at Kuan Tai points to significant event at this time, suggesting a move to another part of the country or further. Seal in Metal at Maturity reveals accumulation of financial security. The Official following Retirement suggests public recognition for career achievements.

from *Ming Shu*
The Art and Practice of Chinese Astrology
Derek Walters/© Pagoda Books

CHINESE HOROSCOPE

Personality Summary
Animal-Type

Time and Date of Birth

Chinese Hour and Date of Birth

| HOUR | DAY | MONTH | YEAR-TYPE |

The Four Pillars

鼠牛虎兔龍蛇
馬羊猴鷄犬豬

Elements for Each Pillar

The Five Elements

WOOD   FIRE   EARTH   METAL   WATER

木火土金水

Fortunate Stems

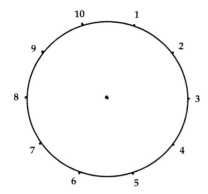

Indications:

Harmonious Branches

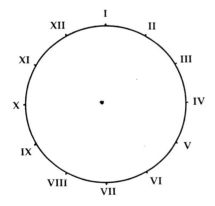

Indications:

The Life-Cycle Chart

	Element		Element
Fate _____		**Wealth** _____	
Seal _____		**Opportunity** _____	
Official _____		**Kuan Tai** _____	

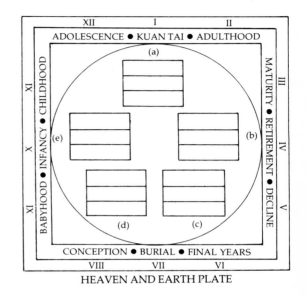

HEAVEN AND EARTH PLATE

Interpretation of the Life-Cycle Chart

from *Ming Shu*
The Art and Practice of Chinese Astrology
Derek Walters/© Pagoda Books

INDEX

FURTHER READING

For more information on ancient
Chinese astrology and horoscopes:
*Chinese Astrology, Interpreting the
Revelations of the Celestial Messengers* by
Derek Walters
Aquarian Press, Wellingborough (1987)

For background reading on
pre-Confucian Chinese beliefs:
Ways to Paradise by Michael Loewe
George Allen & Unwin, London (1979)

For a description of folk customs and life
in modern South-East Asia:
Chinese Creeds and Customs by
V. R. Burkhardt
South China Morning Post, Hong Kong (1982)